LONG ISLAND

Illustrated

ISSUED BY THE TRAFFIC
DEPARTMENT OF THE
LONG ISLAND RAILROAD

Long Island Illustrated
1900
As Published By
The Long Island Railroad

Compiled by
Joel Long & Timothy O. Stuy

International Standard Book Number
978-1-7321191-2-3
Library of Congress Control Number: 2018904576

About this book: This book is a replication of a book originally published by the Long Island Railroad in 1900. It is a guide to the Summer resorts, attractions, and points of interest that could be reached by the LIRR.

Phoebe Snow Company, Inc.™
www.PhoebeSnowCo.com

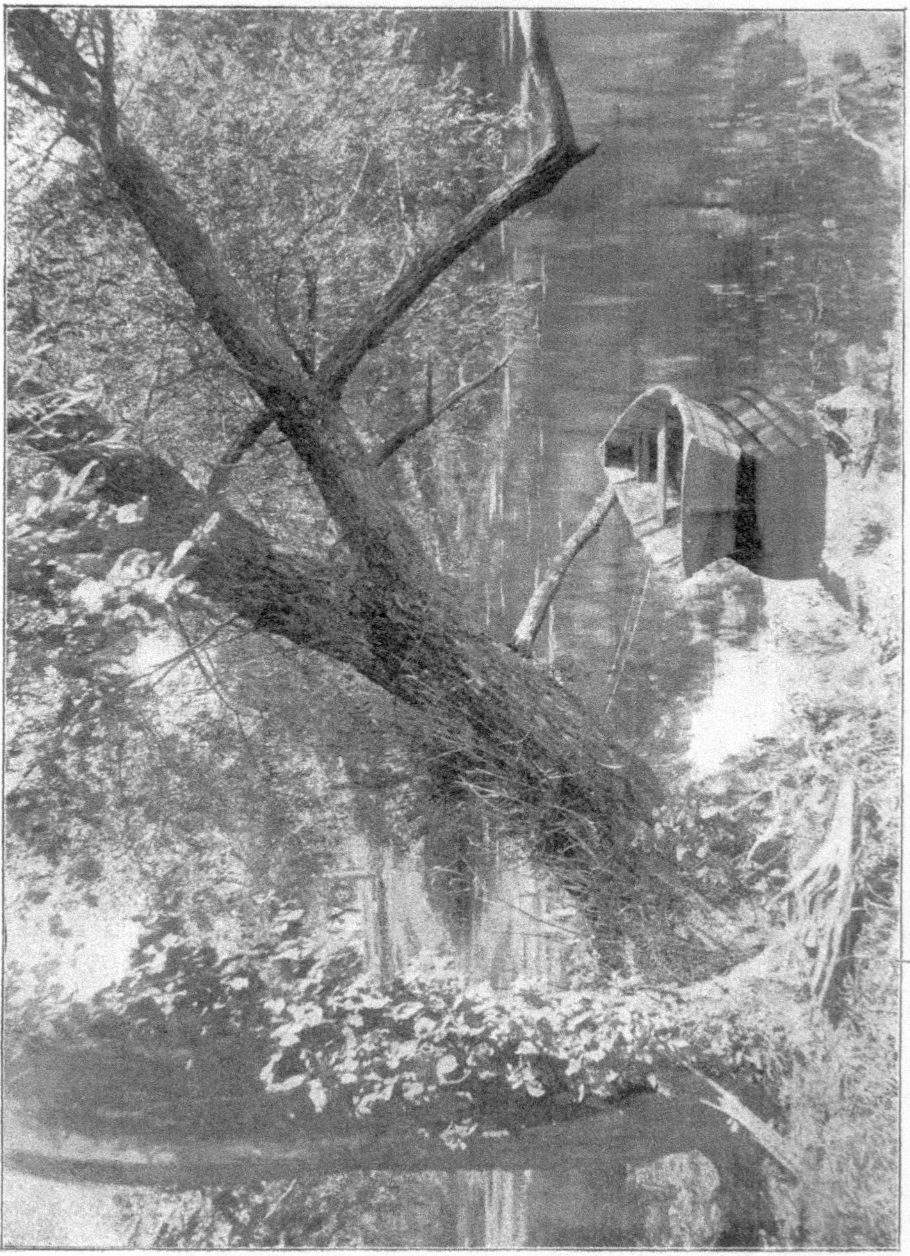

HOW TO REACH LONG ISLAND

T HE Long Island Railroad, by which every important place on Long Island is reached quickly and comfortably, has three terminal stations in the City of New York: one at Long Island City, directly opposite East Thirty-fourth Street, Manhattan Borough; another at Flatbush and Atlantic Avenues, near the heart of the business portion of Brooklyn, and the third in the Eastern District of Brooklyn.

The Long Island City station may be reached from New York by either the ferry from James Slip at the foot of New Chambers Street, or the ferry at the foot of East Thirty-fourth Street. During the summer a steamboat especially adapted to the service is run between Long Island City and Pier 13, near the foot of Wall Street, New York, for the accommodation of downtown business men. This steamboat has a spacious saloon, ample promenade deck, is lighted throughout by electricity, and is a twin-screw propeller, with triple-expansion engines. The station foot of Thirty-fourth Street, East River, is reached by the Second and Third Avenue Elevated Railroads, and by the cross-town street railroads, through transfers, with practically all the city lines.

The Flatbush Avenue station, located in the business portion of Brooklyn Borough, is reached by street cars from New York via the Bridge, and from Fulton and South ferries, and the Pennsylvania Railroad Annex; also by trains on the Fifth Avenue branch of the Elevated Railroad from the Brooklyn Bridge and Fulton Street. All trains starting from this station stop at the Bedford and East New York stations in Brooklyn.

Direct express trains are also run from the Brooklyn Bridge to Jamaica, connecting there with principal trains from uptown New York. Baggage is not carried on these trains.

The Bushwick station is intended for the accommodation of patrons from the Eastern District of Brooklyn, and is reached by surface car lines starting from the Broadway ferries in Brooklyn.

GOLFING ON LONG ISLAND

ESPONDING to the demand for land and space adapted to this royal pastime, we find Long Island in the lead.

In the short space of a few months we have seen magnificent links made over the beautiful Shinnecock Hills, others over the suitable hills upon the Oyster Bay Branch, and in so many other summer resorts on the Island that Long Island is looked upon as the golfing ground of New York. There are links at Amityville, Flushing, Bayside, Port Washington, Richmond Hill, Garden City, Sea Cliff, Nassau (Glen Cove), Oyster Bay, Westbury, Syosset, Cedarhurst, Babylon, Great River, Westhampton, Quogue, Shinnecock Hills, Easthampton and Shelter Island. Out of about one hundred and sixty links in New York State forty are located on Long Island.

LONG ISLAND

FORTUNATE the city which has delightful suburbs. More fortunate still the greater Metropolis which has at its very threshold an expanse of ocean-bounded country where beauty of landscape and health go hand in hand, to which the tired dweller of the city may betake himself for rest, recuperation and recreation, and find the fullest satisfaction.

If New York had nothing else to mark its advantages of location over other cities, it could take pride in the possession

ON THE SOUTH SHORE OF LONG ISLAND

of the ever-beautiful, ever-varied Long Island as one of the most ideal summer breathing places on the American continent. Geographically, Long Island lies between the mighty Atlantic, whose waves surge a never-ending symphony upon the low-lying beaches along its southern shores, and the Sound, that great inland tidal sea, whose surface is ever dotted with the white-winged fleets of commerce. Its ocean coast-line, which is level from Brooklyn to the far-away picturesque Shinnecock Hills, almost at its eastern end, runs nearly east and west, and it is the only section of the United States whose ocean boundaries have this direction. The influence of this peculiarity upon its climate is very marked, as the prevailing winds, wafted over the ocean's surface in summer, are invariably from the south, and they temper the rays of the fiercest midsummer sun.

It is often said of the enterprising American that he takes his pleasures too seriously. It is difficult for him to get away from business, and he carries even into the hours of recreation a suggestion of the counting-room and office. He realizes this himself, for his physician calls it often to his mind. Hence this may account for the fact that he takes his vacation sternly and goes far and spends largely to find it. All foreign countries are picturesque; the novelty exaggerates their characteristics, and to strange eyes the hills of Scotland are of

greater grandeur than the
Catskills, and the moun-
tains of Switzerland more
rugged than the Rockies.
Thus a vacation is alleged
to be more effective if it is
sought at a distance, and
one imagines that he sees
greater wonders in lands
that are new to him,
simply because they are
new. This may explain

ON THE BEACH

the fact that a paradise is neglected in America for a desert
sought in Europe. This is emphasized and increased by a
journey on Long Island. The same sun that gives to Italy
its summer rises from the depths of the waters to set in glow-
ing colors a landscape unsurpassed to eyes wearied by the
ledger and the law book. Try it, you who doubt, and be con-

THE SURF OFF THE HAMPTONS

vinced. Take the train some morning in summer and dis-
cover how close to the noise and bustle of New York is the
glade, the sheltered nook, the green expanse of plain and
the peace and repose of a prosperous and happy country.
Every variety is found in a ride between meals. To the
right as your face is turned eastward is the Great South
Bay, the long stretch of Fire Island, the finest fortification
of nature on the earth, and beyond, old ocean, rolling
breakers in from France. To the north the hills rise

9

gently, until the shores of the placid Sound are a broken series
of parapets lifting themselves like miniature Gibraltars hundreds of feet above the water. One must see it all to fully
enjoy the trip. The scene is full of restful villages with perfect
roads for wheeling, and many places for wayside refreshments
and repose. From the summit of the hills the view extends
for miles. The winds deal gently in summer with the waters,
and there are no storms to buffet the pleasure craft that dot
the scene with their white sails flashing in the sun. As far as
the eye can reach, it is the blue of the waters with the blue of
the sky, softened by a tinge of green for the Connecticut shore
beyond. Few countries offer so charming a vista, none ex-
cel it.

Totally different in appearance, topography, and soil is the
northern shore, which skirts Long Island Sound. Here the
sandy beaches have given way to bold and, in many cases,
precipitous bluffs, into and between which the Sound has
broken and spreads itself out in placid and picturesque bays.
Great arms of this inland sea stretch here and there into the
interior. Upon their shores are charming sites for summer
homes, where the loveliest of marine views may be enjoyed
amid surroundings of field and meadow. The central portion of Long Island partakes of the characteristics of a farming country, in which agriculture has made advanced strides
and been carried to its higher perfection. In soil and climatic
conditions it is admirably adapted to vegetable and fruit farming. Thousands of its broad acres are being scientifically and

intelligently tilled, and from this region there comes to the market of the City of New York daily contributions in enormous volume, and of the finest quality.

In a general way, these are the chief characteristics of the Island, which is the natural summer outlet of the crowded New York. One must be of most exacting taste who cannot find amid the almost infinite variety of charming spots some place which shall possess the desired requisites of a satisfactory summer abiding place.

A close analysis of the three general divisions of Long Island—that is, the seashore, middle, and north shore regions

A FAMILIAR SCENE OFF LONG ISLAND

—discloses what an unusual wealth of attractions each possesses. These are more or less individual, and yet the same dominant chords run in a harmonious unison through all. If one enjoys the sea, with its charms of surf bathing, sailing, and deep-water fishing, there are the many beautiful villages along the south shore. In each of these may be found excellently appointed hotels, and many boarding-houses where accommodations may be had at a less expense. Then there are, nearer by, the great hotels at Manhattan Beach, Arverne, Edgemere, Far Rockaway, and Long Beach, all furnishing the most desirable accommodations, and delightfully located upon

the very edge of the surf. Skirting the southern side of the
Island for nearly eighty miles is the Great South Bay, which
is one of the most ideal and safest places in the wide world
for sailing and still-water bathing. It is the great play-ground
of the smaller yachts, and affords those whose timidity pre-
vents their enjoyment on the ocean or Sound an opportunity
to indulge to the fullest extent in life upon the water, which
is such a charming feature of Long Island summer life. On
a summer's day hundreds of yachts and sailboats may be

WAITING FOR THE EVENING TRAIN TO COME IN

counted skimming over the sparkling surface of the beautiful
bay.

There is room and accommodations upon Long Island for
the millionaire, the man who is well-to-do, and the prudent
wage-earner who must needs get the most comfort for the least
money. In many localities clubs and associations, composed
of wealthy gentlemen, have selected choice sites, and erected
delightful clubhouses, in which they have set up all the
luxuries and conveniences of metropolitan life. Several of
these clubs have purchased or leased large tracts of land

12

ONE OF LONG ISLAND'S PICTURESQUE ROADS

which are held and operated as private shooting preserves. But the territory thus held, compared with the great area of Long Island, is lost sight of in the wealth and variety of what is left. It is in the almost numberless villages, which dot the Island from end to end, that the average person will prefer to make his summer home. The exact location will depend, of course, largely on individual tastes and whether or not daily trips to and from the city must needs be made. There are a score of delightful towns near enough to New York to be of quick access, where hotel accommodations may be had at from $8.00 to $30.00 per week, and board in private houses, either in the towns or upon nearby farms, at from $4.00 per week up. The character and excellence of such accommodations on Long Island are exceptionally good.

In no other region of country is there a greater variety or abundance of those things which "tickle the palate" of mankind. The surrounding waters teem with the finest varieties of salt-water fish, including the world-famous Little Neck clams. The Blue Point oysters are natives of the Great South Bay, on the south side. The Island produces vegetables and fruits in the greatest abundance, and the markets of New York, which are easily accessible, supply the few delicacies for the table that are not raised upon the Island or caught in

OILING THE ROADBED OF THE LONG ISLAND RAILROAD

14

its surrounding waters. Thus it will be seen that the resident of Long Island is likely to have his physical needs well provided for.

To the artist, whether of brush or camera, Long Island offers, not in the sense of time, a new field, yet one which is ever new and fresh in opportunities, and prolific of subjects. Its woodlands, its meadows, its broad level moors, with the bright sea beyond, will challenge the skill of hand and eye as long as art shall last. Its Dutch windmills, choice bits of antiquity and landmarks of other days, have been in the past, and will be in the future, an inspiration for many a canvas. When the sea is boisterous, and is piling in "mountains high," those who love to paint the ocean in its wildest frenzies may

ON MANHATTAN BEACH

have the freest scope for their genius, and perhaps, as is frequently the case, some great ship will be tossed far up on the beach, and the sturdy life-savers from one of the numerous stations which dot the shore will become living models for a thrilling chef-d'œuvre.

While the south shore of Long Island is almost at the doorway of New York City, the difference in its temperature is most marked. Only those who have sweltered in the city and then gone out into one of the charming towns along the ocean side of the Island, to find it so cool at night that a blanket "feels good," can realize the great, almost phenomenal, difference in the temperature. Here there are no towering piles of brick and mortar which store the heat by day to give it out at night; but, rather, broad stretches of daisy-

READY FOR THE RUN

grown meadowlands and well-tilled fields to add a touch of fragrance to the ocean's cooling breeze.

These suburban places on Long Island offer the only opportunity to business men who must needs be at their desks daily through the summer months, of locating their families where they may have all the desirable advantages of the seashore, and where they themselves may spend each night without making the daily journey to and from the city a tiresome, wearying feature of the summer. For those to whom daily trips to the city are not necessary, or for that larger body of business men who locate their families in some pleasant place and join them over every Sunday, the eastern end of Long Island spreads out an inviting list of places. Among them are Moriches, Westhampton, Quogue, Good Ground, Shinnecock Hills, Southampton, Bridgehampton, Easthampton, Amagansett, Montauk, Sag Harbor, and the popular and always delightful Shelter Island, with its charming surroundings and excellent hotels, and the delightful resorts, River Head, Jamesport, Mattituck, Cutchogue, Southold, of the Long Island Railroad, on beautiful Peconic Bay.

16

During the past few years, many miles of the main line have been relaid with heavy steel rails, new coaches have been added, and new hard-coal burning locomotives placed in service, thus reducing the annoyance from smoke.

More than twelve hundred trains are operated on Long Island daily, and six hundred and fifty arrive and depart from Brooklyn and Long

THE FIRST LESSON

Island City during the summer. With such an array of natural advantages, its proximity to New York, and the exceptionally fine facilities of transportation and inter-communication, Long Island may properly be called the ideal summer territory of the Union. It is furnishing homes each year for a larger throng. Its popularity has spread far beyond the limits of Greater New York, and an ever-increasing percentage of its summer residents are coming from the Middle, Southern, and Western States, as they find within its borders all the requisites of a delightful summer-land. But not only does Long Island appeal to the summer resident. It is as well an ideal place in which is established a permanent suburban home. Its nearness to New York, the superiority of its railroad service, the excellence of its school system, and the high quality of its society, all unite in producing conditions which are most eagerly sought by those who wish to establish a home of their own outside of the limited confines of the city. Long Island is known everywhere as the Cyclers' Paradise. The splendid roads of the north and south shores, the great number of beautiful cycle paths and smooth hard-edge paths, make unsurpassed wheeling. While the hilly country of the north shore gives the tourist climbs, coasts,

17

and extended views, the level south shore makes long trips a matter of little exertion and affords innumerable glimpses of inlets, bays, and the ocean. There has been in the recent past the greatest activity in road improvement all over the island; there are now more than six hundred miles of macadamized thoroughfares. Besides this, there are hundreds of miles of well-graded and excellently maintained bicycle paths for the use of wheelmen, for whom Long Island is a paradise. Many of these paths follow most picturesque roads, under the grateful shade of overhanging oaks, giving here and there lovely vistas of the blue ocean, and broader views of the rolling fields and attractive villages. So many thousands of wheelmen have come to realize the delights of the Island that the railroad will this year again run special bicycle cars attached to certain trains, so that a tour may be begun or finished at any place desired.

Excellent accommodations can be found everywhere on the Island, and the majority of the inns and hotels cater to the cycling public.

The many sections of the Good Roads Association constantly keep roads and paths in good condition, and the signboards erected by the L. A. W. giving directions and distances make touring on the Island a comfort not known in any section of the United States.

The Long Island Railroad Company was the first railroad in the United States to build and equip special bicycle cars with the very best appliances for the transportation of bicycles without injury.

The "Cyclists' Paradise," a small handbook issued by the Long Island Railroad Company, has a good map of the roads and paths of Long Island, together with tables of distances, railroad time-tables, hotel lists, suggestions, and, in fact, complete information in condensed form. This book will be sent to any address upon receipt of two-cent stamp to cover postage.

Long Island is particularly fortunate in having the service of the New York and New Jersey Telephone Company, which practically reaches the uttermost parts of the Island. Exchanges or Pay Stations are now located in almost all of the towns and villages from Brooklyn eastward, as well as in the stations of the Long Island Railroad Company, thus placing the residents within easy touch with each other and with the points they most need to reach, as well as making it possible for them to communicate with all the places in the vast telephone system—Chicago, Boston, St. Louis, being brought within as easy speaking range as New York or Brooklyn. Pay stations are located in many of the summer resort hotels, so that the guest from town may receive news from his office and transmit hourly instructions thereto, if need be. Probably no one more thoroughly appreciates the value and convenience of telephone service than the business man who is out of town for the summer, or whose family sojourns at the seaside while he remains in town, the telephone service making easy communication possible. The value of telephone service in social matters is strongly felt in the summer, in obtaining information as to trains and boats, calling one's friends and engaging them for occasions, instructing sailing masters, ordering carriages, and making easy the many other details of social life. As an element of safety and in an emergency, the telephone service is invaluable. The physician may be summoned, police aid called, or a fire alarm sent more speedily than by any other means. To the broker, banker, or merchant, the telephone brings the latest news from headquarters as nothing else can, keeps him in touch with the market quotations, and saves him much travel and endless vexation. It enables him to inform his family instantly and surely if he be detained in town, and also to learn if anything of importance may necessitate a change of his plans. The telephone service of to-day places the patron on Long Island, through the New York and New Jersey Telephone Company's system, in communication if need be with any of the fifty-five thousand stations on and around Long Island, the City of New York, and nearby cities and towns, and with over two hundred thousand telephone stations throughout the country through the Long Distance lines. The general offices of the New York and New Jersey Telephone Company are at 81 Willoughby Street, Brooklyn, while an office at Riverhead, L. I., furnishes any information desired in that section of Long Island. In the following pages will be found a brief mention of the various localities and towns upon Long Island.

SHORE RESORTS NEAR NEW YORK

A T the very threshold of the greatest metropolis on this continent is what may be truly called the greatest seaside resort in the world. One is hardly out of the suburbs of one until he is in the heart of the other. It is but a step from the noise and turmoil of the city to the silvery sands which edge the majestic Atlantic, from the discordant notes of trade and commerce to the musical surgings of the "ever-sounding" sea.

In Manhattan Beach, New York has a breathing place which has grown into the greatest popularity, not through the artifices of adroit advertising, but by reason of the merits of its own attractiveness. It is no longer necessary for those who live in the city of New York to make long journeys to find delightful seaside conditions. They are but thirty minutes away from the downtown business district. Two great hotels furnish most excellent accommodations, the Manhattan and the Oriental. The latter is entirely apart from the portion of the beach patronized by transients, and is one of the most delightful houses on the Atlantic coast. It is said that none other has had as guests so many distinguished people. The service and cuisine of the Oriental are as perfect as unlimited means and good taste can make them. Perfect rest and quiet may be enjoyed here, and seashore life enjoyed under the most favorable conditions. The Oriental has along

HUNTING SEASHORE SHELLS

20

MANHATTAN BEACH HOTEL AND THE THEATRE

its front handsome, wide, well-shaded verandas, which look out across the beautiful lawns and flower beds to the ocean, which is but a few steps away. Its public rooms are pleasingly furnished, and its rooms bright and cheerful. The hotel meets admirably in every particular the designs of its promoter, which were that it should furnish the highest type of accommodations, and be an agreeable home for its guests rather than a resort for the multitude.

The Manhattan is an immense and impressive structure, built close up to the ocean side. Its wide, well-shaded verandas, of almost endless length, make a most charming open-air café, where thousands of city dwellers gather every evening to enjoy the excellent cuisine, listening meanwhile to the sweet strains of music which float out from the nearby theatre. A more fascinating scene is difficult to imagine than that presented at Manhattan Beach every afternoon and evening. It is not to be compared to any other, for there is none like it. There is in it a little glimpse of Paris, a suggestion of the happy throngs, the brilliant lights, and touches of gay color one finds at the cafés along the Bois de Boulogne, and there is that, too, which recalls the attractions of Ostend and Brighton, or of the charming Lido on the Adriatic at Venice. But, after all, it is Manhattan Beach, happy and proud in a character and charm all its own. Directly in front of the Manhattan and separated from it by brightened flower-beds and velvety lawns is the great board walk, hanging in places almost over the surf, which pounds unceasingly, as if determined to batter all barriers, against the strong bulwarks of piling. This walk furnishes a most delightful promenade, where the purest of sea air may be enjoyed without contamination of any sort, and where the view is unobstructed to the horizon's farthest line. Adjoining the Manhattan is the large theatre, so constructed as to be "swept by ocean breezes." Here during the entire season are concerts or operas both afternoon and evening.

The usual attractions will prevail at "The Beach." The opera season will be as pleasing as heretofore; nothing will be left undone to secure the highest type of entertainment, and to maintain the enviable standard already reached.

The great bathing pavilion adjoins the beach, and here, as everywhere at Manhattan Beach, the arrangements for furnishing the best accommodations are noticeable. Suits in abundance may be obtained, and, high tide or low tide, it matters not, there is always a happy throng disporting themselves in the surf. Life lines are stretched so as to enclose ample space, which is safe, and stalwart life-savers are ever drifting in boats along the outer edge, ready to give immediate help to any who may have been foolish enough to have gone beyond their depth or strength.

A brilliant entertainment provided at Manhattan Beach after the dinner hour is the Fire Drama and Pyrotechnic Display by Pain. It is given in an immense enclosure in the rear of the Manhattan Hotel, and here on an enormous stage, with an artificial lake in front and vast walls of scenery be-

SATURDAY AFTERNOON AT THE SHORE

hind, are enacted spectacular and vivid reproductions of stirring historical events. The brilliancy of these displays baffles adequate description. The plot, if such it can be called, is usually warlike, and includes the capture of some apparently impregnable fortress. Thousands of rockets, bombs, and brilliant pyrotechnic inventions are set off. The attack, the repulse, and ultimate victory of the great army of men and detachments of cavalry, who march and counter-march, and finally capture the fortress, are exciting in the extreme. When the moment of victory comes, the whole air seems filled with bursting bombs, and at last the entire fabric of scenery bursts into flame, and peace comes amid wild, tumultuous detonations and a veritable shower of golden sparks. Hundreds of

23

BATHING ON THE LONG ISLAND BEACHES

people are employed
in this wonderfully
brilliant production,
and the heavens are
made bright with the
a l m o s t continuous
a n d e v e r-beautiful
fire constellations of
red, blue, green, and
gold.

To the west of the
fireworks enclosure
and in the rear of the
Manhattan is the bi-
cycle track, with its
well-laid c e m e n t
roadway, one-third of
a mile around and

HARDLY ROOM FOR ONE MORE

flanked by extensive grand stands. This course has been the
scene of many of the most interesting of America's racing
events, and as there is a superb track leading to it, it has become a popular rendezvous for thousands of wheelmen and
wheelwomen, who may enjoy a spin on their wheels, a bath in
the surf, and then make the outing complete by dining sump-
tuously at the Manhattan.

New Yorkers have always shown their great appreciation of
the enterprise of the management of Manhattan Beach in providing thoroughly high-class musical entertainments by most
liberal patronage. Not only has the music been exceptionally
fine, but the opportunity of combining the seashore and opera
is only presented at Manhattan. No form of summer evening
entertainments has greater charms than those which attach to
dining at Manhattan Beach, and then hearing a bright, pretty
opera well rendered in a vast auditorium which is fanned by
the ever-cooling breezes of old ocean, whose surf is breaking
almost under the very eaves of the open-air structure. Surely
under such influence "Cares which infest the day shall fold
their tents like the Arabs, and as silently steal away."

At Sheepshead Bay, which is a neighbor of Manhattan
Beach, is located the race track of the Coney Island Jockey
Club, one of the best known and successful racing associations

25

in the country. This resort enjoys a large and select patronage, and its natural location, surrounded as it is by forests, and cooled by the ocean breezes, makes it very popular. On such occasions as the Suburban Stakes day many thousands gather at this course, the railroad facilities being so perfect that they go or come with little or no inconvenience. Another successful racing association near by is the Brooklyn Jockey Club, upon whose track at Gravesend the Handicap Stakes is one of the chief events.

Following the coast line to the east, the next resort reached is Rockaway Beach, which is upon a long peninsula stretching out between the ocean on the one side and Jamaica Bay on the other. This beach is in reality but a continuation of the long lone if low-lying keys which skirt the entire south side of Long Island. Farther up toward the point of the peninsula is Rockaway Park, with its many attractive homes. It is a particularly healthful and delightful spot, being almost entirely encompassed by water, and offering the advantages of seclusion, and of both surf and still-water bathing.

And beyond them the modern summer city-by-the-sea, Arverne. Here is located a superb hotel surrounded by a twenty-foot veranda, and with accommodations for over four hundred guests. By a happy architectural treatment, the hotel is so constructed that every room looks out directly upon the ocean. The town of Arverne has been laid out with streets

SNIPE SHOOTING ON LONG ISLAND

COTTAGES AT ARVERNE-BY-THE-SEA

ARVERNE HOTEL, ARVERNE-BY-THE-SEA

and avenues stretching from the sea to the bay. These are
broad and well improved, and trees have been planted along
them to provide shade. The summer population of Arverne
is five thousand and rapidly increasing. Many handsome summer homes, which bespeak the taste of their owners, have
been erected at Arverne, and a large number of wealthy people spend the summer here. In addition to the large hotel,
there are a number of smaller ones, and a sufficient number of
boarding-houses to care for the large summer population.
Social life at Arverne is very gay. There is much driving, and
scores of elegant equipages may be seen any pleasant afternoon upon the avenues and drives. Bathing is, of course, the
chief recreation, but all kinds of out-of-door exercise are
popular. Few places on the coast out-rival Arverne in attractive appearance.

Beyond Arverne to the east is the magnificent new hotel,
the Edgemere, which has taken, as it deserved to, a position
among America's most delightful summer hotels. It is modern
in style and construction, and perfect in detail, furnishings,
and equipment, and has accommodations for four hundred
guests. It stands near the ocean and commands a charming
view from its great verandas and living-rooms.

Among the resorts which were popular a generation ago
and which have held their own in public esteem must be
counted Far Rockaway. The glare and the enterprise of the
more modern resorts have not overshadowed it, and it still
enjoys a large patronage and takes on many material aspects

28

A BIT OF THE BEAUTIFUL AND PICTURESQUE ROCKAWAY BEACH

not possessed by other places on the Island, and attracts each season an immense number of visitors who find it one of the most delightful of all Long Island's resorts. It possesses every characteristic of an ideal place for a sojourn of a day or a season. Near by it and on the same peninsula is Wave Crest, with many handsome cottages and beautiful lawns. Much public interest is manifested in keeping the streets and walks in perfect condition. While Wave Crest is in Far Rockaway, it is entirely distinct from it, and maintains its individuality rigorously. Bayswater, a neighbor of Wave Crest, is another exceedingly attractive place.

Adjoining Far Rockaway is Lawrence, which the wealth of its residents has made to "blossom like a rose." The attention which has been paid to the æsthetic features of Lawrence are immediately noticeable to the visitor. In its charming lawns, beautiful trees, and ornamental floriculture, it suggests Newport. It further suggests the possibility of improvement which exists in almost all small villages, where the

citizens unite enthusiastically and earnestly in an effort to
make all things pleasing to the eye. The village of Lawrence
has an attractive clubhouse, with a large number of members
among the best class of cottage residents. Its schools are also
of the very best. Lawrence is a delightfully healthful location
for permanent residents. Its remarkable accessibility to the
shores of the Atlantic Ocean, its easy touch with New York
or Brooklyn, its essentially rural situation combined with the
splendid service of more than thirty trains each way every
week-day over the Long Island Railroad—all have a strong
tendency to make Lawrence one of the most charming all-
the-year-around residential sections of Long Island. The
immediate section hereabouts is noted for the peculiar purity
and its air, and the wholesomeness of the surroundings.

A CAPTURE ON THE LONG ISLAND SHORE

Further inland, on the broad neck of land which terminates in the Rockaways, is Cedarhurst, a private residential reservation, with exclusive tendencies, and a beautiful clubhouse. Many miles of road have been laid out and improved, through the natural and extensive groves of cedars, pines, maples, and oaks, and the natural advantages and scenery greatly improved by the expenditure of a considerable amount of money. In every way that good taste can indicate, the best results have been attained in making the region attractive and beautiful. The members of the association find their enjoyment in wholesome out-of-door games and sports, and in the attractions of the club. There are large stables for the polo ponies, for this game is one of the most popular at Cedarhurst, kennels for the hounds, and a well-equipped gymnasium for the members who prefer to take this manner of exercise. In addition to all these, there are golf links, shooting preserves, etc. The hunts and runs of the club are famous as being picturesque and Englishesque, and always afford the greatest enjoyment to those who are "lookers-on in Venice," as well as participants. Cedarhurst, Woodmere, and Hewletts are on the line of the Long Island Railroad which leaves the south shore main line at Valley Stream and runs out onto the Rockaway Peninsula. At Woodmere there is a notable avenue one hundred feet wide, which is delightfully shaded and improved on either side by many handsome residences. Hewletts, the neighbor of Woodmere on the north, is an attractive little village amid surroundings of a pleasing rural nature.

The trains of the main line division of the Long Island Railroad, whether leaving from the Brooklyn or Long Island City terminals, pass through Jamaica, which is practically the hub of the system.

Following the south shore line east from Jamaica, the first village reached is Springfield, which takes its name from the springs of crystal water bursting forth from their subterranean sources here, one of them being so large as to form quite a pretentious lake. Rosedale, the next village to the east, is a brisk and enterprising little place, with charming surroundings of woodland and meadow. Its nearest neighbor is Valley Stream, the junction for the Far Rockaway branch. The north and south line, starting at Oyster Bay on the north shore and continuing through Nassau, Glen Cove, Roslyn,

A WRECK, WITH BREECHES BUOY, JUST AFTER THE RESCUE

Mineola, Garden City and Hempstead, also unites with the south shore line at Valley Stream.

A portion of the trains for Far Rockaway run by the way of Valley Stream, while others go via the New York & Rockaway Beach Railway. This enables the visitor to go one way and return by the other, thus adding to the variety and enjoyment of the journey. The route via Woodhaven Junction takes the traveler across the beautiful Jamaica Bay over the long trestles which stretch from one island to the other. Upon either side of the train the immediate view is over sparkling waves, which add a touch of salt to the cooling breeze wafted into the open windows.

This experience of railroading on the water is so refreshing that one is tempted to wish that the journey was thrice as long. Continuing beyond Valley Stream we come to Lynbrook, which is the junction point for East Rockaway and Long Beach. Here a branch of the south shore division of the Long Island Railroad turns toward the ocean, and, crossing the

THE LONG BEACH HOTEL

beautiful Hempstead Bay at its narrowest point, terminates at the very door of the immense Long Beach Hotel. This is one of the largest and most attractive of America's ocean-side hotels. It has accommodations for a thousand guests and a large casino, and a number of cottages have been erected near the main house, where much lower rates of board prevail. It is one of the most popular of New York suburban summer hotels, and in addition to the enjoyments of bathing, there is a constant variety of entertainments provided at the hotel for the enjoyment of the guests.

The Long Beach Hotel drawing-room and ballroom offer daily and nightly attractions to the guests. The morning concerts, given by a superb orchestra, take place on the spacious veranda at this end of the hotel, and each evening the gay strains of the waltz or two-step tempt the hearer to try a "pas deux" on the polished floor of the great dance hall. During the hour of the morning concert a kindergarten, under an admirable teacher, provides entertainment for the little ones.

The beach, which is directly in front of the hotel, is hard and clean, and the slope is so slight that it makes bathing safe and enjoyable. Every precaution is taken by the management against accidents, and a competent corps of life-savers is always in attendance. Upon summer days hundreds of people are in the surf during the bathing hours, and the scene is one of greatest gaiety. Sailing and fishing, both upon the ocean or the quiet waters of Hempstead Bay, are, with surf bathing, the popular features of life at Long Beach.

East Rockaway, situated on an arm of the bay, is a quiet place, within a few minutes' ride of Long Beach. A few miles

33

farther east is Rockville Centre, a town of considerable importance as a local trade centre. It has many attractive homes and good schools, including a fine High School. Rockville Centre has not opened its doors very wide as yet to summer boarders, not because of lack of hospitality on the part of its residents, but chiefly because of lack of hotel accommodations, but its splendid location and proximity to the city is certain to insure a rapid growth.

Baldwins, just beyond Rockville Centre, is identified by the graceful spire of the village church, which adds a picturesque background to the beautiful perspective of the surrounding fields. It is an inviting settlement, in which peace and happiness abound. That it is growing is evident from the many improvements under way.

WOODCLEFT INN AT FREEPORT

Freeport bears on its very face the always distinguishable marks of prosperity. It is a town of comfortable and attractive homes, well-stocked shops, and fine churches. It has an exceptionally good society, and is the home of many well-to-do people, who have demonstrated their æsthetic tastes by creating two town parks, which are kept in excellent condition. An attractive hotel, the Woodcleft Inn, is located at Freeport. It has accommodations for one hundred and twenty guests, and is well managed. The country around Freeport, and through which the railroad passes, is one of great natural attractiveness and beauty. It is dry and rolling, and hence healthy. Its gentle slope is toward the sea, from which there is, during the summer season, an ever-refreshing and tonic-laden breeze. A newly erected railroad station, handsome and commodious, just completed, adds very materially to the comfort and convenience of passengers.

Merrick, the next station beyond Freeport, is chiefly known because of its extensive camp-meeting grounds. Here is also located a model farm, dairy, and trout preserves.

Bellmore, Wantagh, and Seaford lie to the east of Merrick, and in each of these there are a number of attractive homes, with ample open-air surroundings, and no appearance of over-crowding. They are near enough to the Great South Bay to catch the odor of the salty sedges which edge its shore, and yet far enough away to be on high, healthy ground.

Massapequa, which assumed a new name (it was formerly South Oyster Bay) with its modern prosperity, has, in addition to its excellent and inviting hotel, the Massapequa, a goodly number of modern, up-to-date summer cottages, occupied largely by their owners. These are surrounded by velvety

MASSAPEQUA HOTEL

35

lawns, and they bespeak the select character of the residents. One of the most attractive stations on the line of the railroad has been built at Massapequa, and there are in the village several good churches and schools. A salt-water creek meanders up through the meadows from the bay almost to the entrance of the excellent Massapequa Hotel, so that ready access may be had to the bay and ocean.

Amityville is a thrifty, progressive little city, full of push and energy, and abreast with all the modernisms usually found in a place of its population, which is about three thousand. It has several good hotels, among which the New Point is the newest and most complete. It is thoroughly attractive

NEW POINT HOTEL, AMITYVILLE

and handsomely furnished, and is the centre of a most delightful social circle each season. It has electric lights and gas, and its streets are well graded and beautified by countless trees. It is one of the chief resorts on Long Island, and deserves its signal success in this line, for it has all the features desirable in a summer resort. Both the marine and land views are inviting, and the town and hotels are so close to the water that sailing and bathing are the dominating pleasures. The golf links here are deservedly popular. Directly across the bay from Amityville is the Gilgo Inlet, through which sailboats pass out into the ocean, where there is deep-sea fishing of the finest kind. Every day a large fleet of pleasure boats are to be seen passing in and out, filled with people enjoying the sport.

SAILING ON THE GREAT SOUTH BAY

All along this section of the south shore of Long Island the water front has been largely taken up by those owning their own homes, or by investment companies which are spending money liberally in developing the property, and making it desirable and available for cottage sites. For this purpose it is particularly well adapted, as it is not only easy of access from the city, but is healthy, free from malarial influences, and is always delightfully cool in summer, as its location is such that it has the benefit of direct ocean breezes. All of these advantages have resulted in making this section exceedingly popular with those who enjoy suburban life.

ARGYLE LAKE AND HOTEL, BABYLON

Passing through Lindenhurst, Babylon is reached. It is one of the most popular as well as one of the most attractive of the score or more of south shore villages. It includes, besides its permanent residences, a large colony of beautiful summer cottage homes, many of them suggesting in style and taste the wealth of their owners. There are first-class hotels here, among them a handsome modern hotel, the Argyle, surrounded by exquisite lawn effects. The Watson House also is a thoroughly comfortable and commodious hotel, and has much prestige in a long-established and well-earned reputation. The town has many up-to-date features, such as gas works, and electric light plant, social clubs, well-stocked shops, game preserves, and other attractions. Its churches are numerous and prosperous, and its citizens enterprising.

Located directly upon the Great South Bay, it enjoys both by day and night the cool and invigorating breezes which come directly from the ocean. The scene at the railroad station upon the arrival of the afternoon trains from New York is a brilliant one, as the open space adjoining the station is filled with handsome equipages, with liveried attendants, and gaily dressed ladies awaiting the arrival of fathers, husbands, and sweethearts from the city.

In this respect and in many others Babylon is like Newport and a few of the other select American shore resorts. The visitor will be charmed on every hand by the quiet and unostentatious display of wealth, refinement, and comfort. The Westminster Kennel Club, located at Babylon, attracts each season many people of the highest social distinction, who enjoy bringing the element of sport into their summer life, and who by so doing add a variety and gaiety to the society of the place. The golf links afford much pleasure, and enter heartily into competition for precedence with the many diversities and out-of-door sports.

Opposite Babylon, on Muncie Island, is the Muncie Surf Sanitarium. There is a quiet home atmosphere about the place that is contagious, restful, and strengthening. Then fresh breezes from the ocean forever blow here and every breath is a tonic.

A steam launch is run between Babylon and Muncie Island, making two trips daily and carrying the mails.

From Babylon, Oak Island Beach is reached by steamer. Near this place are the headquarters of the jovial Wawayanda and Short Beach clubs, each having a large membership among New York and Brooklyn business men, and the well-known Armory of Jesse Smith.

Returning to the main island and continuing eastward from Babylon, the traveler comes first to Bayshore, which, with its fine churches, handsome residences, and parked grounds, its prosperous stores, good schools, and broad, well-kept roadways, always makes a most favorable impression. Bay-

ARRIVAL OF THE EXPRESS AT BAYSHORE

shore is a suitable all-the-year-around town, to which the summer cottage feature is but a pleasing addition. It is a town which even the casual visitor can see offers comfort and opportunities for a delightful existence. The handsome cot-

PROSPECT HOUSE, BAYSHORE

tage homes with their broad verandas and wide-stretching lawns indicate that the residents of the village have as a class a refined taste and an inclination to make their homes and town expressive of that refinement. Some of the handsomest houses on Long Island are located at Bayshore, as well as the large grounds of the Bayshore Driving Park Association and the attractive property of the Olympic Club. Driving and wheeling are popular pastimes, for the roads are delightful. There are good hotels at Bayshore, among them the well-known and always popular Prospect House, which is modernly appointed and enjoys a large and select patronage. Directly across the Great South Bay from Bayshore, and reached by steamer, is the far-famed

PROSPECT HOUSE, COTTAGES AND GROUNDS AT BAYSHORE

Fire Island, whose lighthouse is known the maritime world over as the place from whence all transatlantic steamships are first sighted and their arrival telegraphed to New York. This island is a low-lying sand key, not over a mile in width at any one point, and full forty in length. It forms a natural breakwater for the south shore of Long Island, and between it and the main shore is the Great South Bay so frequently referred to in this book. Some years ago the island was purchased by New York, and although several syndicates have undertaken its purchase, it still remains one of the State's possessions.

The great lighthouse, whose electric beacon of twenty-three million candle-power is the most powerful in the country, is a never-ending source of interest to visitors. It is an immense structure, and its friendly light, which is plainly visible for many miles at sea, has brought joy and comfort to many a storm-tossed mariner.

Farther up the island toward the east is the new settlement of Point o'Woods, which is called the Long Island Chautauqua Assembly. There is a fine auditorium here with seating capacity of several thousand, and a group of comfortable cottages. During the season there are daily entertainments, also lectures on interesting and instructive topics by well-known authorities. Point o'Woods may be reached direct by steamer from Bayshore.

Islip, which was settled originally by a goodly people from Islip, Oxfordshire, England, the near neighbor of Bayshore on the east, is quite like it in its surroundings. It has a small resident population, but a large one during the summer, when the magnificent country houses located here are occupied by the families of their wealthy owners. There are at Islip a number of well-kept hotels. From the settlement beautiful views may be enjoyed of the Great South Bay, and the wooded points which stretch out like the fingers of the hand from the main shore.

The portion of Long Island which skirts the south shore hereabouts is heavily covered with pine forests, which give the air the double advantage of the odor of the balsam and the tonic of the sea. It is a region which duplicates in general appearances and climatic effects Lakewood, N. J., but with added advantages of being much nearer New York and more easily and comfortably reached. Through this forest growth the roads run in every direction, and add to the delights of outdoor life by making riding and bicycling charming pastimes.

New York millionaires have been quick to realize that this immediate locality was an ideal one for the location of their summer homes, and as a consequence there are a large number of extensive estates, magnificent in both the area included and in development. One of the most notable of these is the place of Mr. W. K. Vanderbilt, at Oakdale. His estate includes a portion of what is known as the old Nichols grant, whose ownership runs back two centuries. There is also the immense and almost royal estate of Mr. F. G. Bourne, upon which many thousands of dollars have been spent in the handsome villa and in the improvement of the grounds. In addition to these is another, the Cutting estate, equally beautiful and extensive.

The Vanderbilt estate, which is enclosed by a high iron fence, is entered by a beautiful ornamental gate, at the side of which is a picturesque ivy-covered porter's lodge. Just outside the gate, at the side of the old post road, which is the most popular bicycle thoroughfare out of New York, is a deep well of the purest water. This well is known to thousands of wheelmen, who have stopped to quench their thirst and rest under the refreshing shade of the enormous wide-spreading elms which surround it. Frequently on holidays and pleasant summer Saturday afternoons as many as a hundred bicyclists may be counted here at one time, with many more coming and going continually.

Near the Vanderbilt estate, with Oakdale as the railroad station, are the handsome quarters and preserves of the famous South Side Sportsman's Club, an institution of great popularity and enviable repute. Its membership includes many well-known New Yorkers and during the spring, summer and fall the clubhouse is the centre of continued gaiety. A large number of deer and an infinite variety of smaller game are killed here every autumn.

The nearby St. John's Church, which is the fashionable place to attend divine service, has been in existence more than one hundred and thirty years.

BATHING PIER AT SAYVILLE

43

Sayville is justly one of the most populous and popular villages on the south shore. It adjoins Oakdale on the east and has innumerable advantages and attractions. The town has a considerable permanent population and many well-stocked shops. There are several attractive hotels near the bay-side. The Elmore is not only charmingly located, but is well kept, and has accommodations for more than one hun-

SCENES AT SAYVILLE

dred guests, many of whom return year after year for the entire season. It is near the water, and the bathing-grounds are surrounded by beautiful and well-shaded lawns. Sayville has many beautiful cottages with highly improved surroundings, and the railroad facilities are so excellent that many New York business men go in and out every day. The surrounding woodlands are kept in perfect condition, and are in reality private parks in which trespassing is forbidden, although summer visitors have no difficulty in obtaining permission to enjoy them. Between Sayville and Blue Point, the home of the oyster famous to epicureans the world around, are the scientific trout ponds of Mr. R. B. Roosevelt, and near by is the little village of Bayport, which, being in a somewhat open country, affords more extended and beautiful views, both over the sedges and bay and far inland over the fertile fields and meadows. The village streets are fascinatingly beautiful, with their grand old elms and comfortable, old-fashioned homes.

THE BEAUTIFUL WEST LAKE AT PATCHOGUE

Patchogue takes on far more metropolitan airs and advantages than any of the towns on the south shore. It has about six thousand inhabitants, and is enjoying a sturdy, wholesome growth. The visitor will be impressed with the city common and the handsome soldiers' monument in its centre, as well as with its many excellent stores, handsome churches, beautiful homes, and the general atmosphere of thrift and enterprise which everywhere predominates. Its streets are broad and well shaded, are lighted with electricity and the place is kept in touch with New York by a number of trains each way.

45

FAMILIAR SCENES AT PATCHOGUE

Patchogue has more of the characteristic features of a popular summer resort than any other place on Long Island. It reminds the visitor who sees it for the first time of Asbury Park, N. J. Its summer population runs into thousands, and there are countless comfortable boarding-houses in addition to good hotels. Patchogue is well known as the headquarters for the throngs of bicyclists who make the fifty-mile run from Jamaica to Patchogue along the magnificent path which skirts

CLIFTON HOUSE AND THE MAIN STREET, PATCHOGUE

the old post-road. One of the chief industries of the place is its oyster trade, thousands of barrels being shipped from here and the neighboring places to European and American markets. There are several flourishing manufacturing establishments here, among them being some extensive lace mills, employing a large number of people.

Patchogue has for years been a famous resort for both fishing and boating, and its water-front, along which there are casinos, bathing pavillions, and other conveniences, is gay at all hours of the day. A very large fleet of excellent sailboats make Patchogue their headquarters all the year round, so that there are always abundant opportunities for either sailing or fishing.

Every one who has listened to the aboriginal names of Long Island localities, or read the story of its early days, will recognize "Patchogue" as Indian. History tells us that more than twelve tribes, who were in their time numerous and powerful, have left their names indelibly stamped on Long Island. They include the Canarsies, the Rockaways, Massapequas, Patchogues, Shinnecocks, Montauks, Manhassets, Amagansetts, Ronkonkomas, and others.

47

FROM PATCHOGUE TO SAG HARBOR AND MONTAUK

THE eastern portion of the south shore of Long Island has been for generations a magnet of attraction to all who "loved nature for nature's sake." In the early days of the century a regular stage route was maintained from Brooklyn to Easthampton. According to the old handbills, a few of which are still in existence, the stage left Brooklyn Court House every Thursday at 9 a. m. It was due at the tavern in Hempstead for dinner and a change of horses, reaching Babylon in the evening and "putting up" there for the night. Friday night was spent at Quogue, and the stage rolled up to the tavern at Easthampton, the end of its journey. Saturday afternoon, having made the one hundred and ten miles in three days. Mark the contrast: To-day the cottager at the far end of the island drops into an easy seat in a handsomely appointed express train at Long Island City or Brooklyn, and with the beauties of the whirling panorama to divide his attention with his newspaper, covers the same distance in less than three hours. Such are the changes of the times.

Bellport has a higher elevation than any of the south shore towns, and for this reason considerable development is anticipated here. Bellport has hotel accommodations for two thousand guests, and many charming homes. The Great South Bay at this point is three miles wide, which gives ample opportunity for sailing and fishing.

Brookhaven, which, because of intervening woodlands, is hidden from the railroad, lies immediately on the shore of the bay, which at this point narrows considerably, so that the "ceaseless song of the mighty surf" is distinctly audible as it rushes up on the narrow outer island. There are in the neighborhood a large number of trout streams, which offer inviting sport in the proper season, and in the fall more game is

48

brought in here from the surrounding region than comes to any place within equal distance from New York. The well-known Suffolk Club, having a large membership made up of prominent New York and Brooklyn gentlemen, is located here and enjoys great popularity.

Mastic is a quiet little place, where the tired man or woman may find the same rest and recreation and under practically the same conditions as he or she finds them in the Adirondack wilderness.

Moriches, a charming summering place down by the bay-side, and a mile from the station of the railroad, is the first important settlement beyond Patchogue. Stages meet every train and convey passengers to any portion of the village, which, with orchards, fields, and meadows intermingled, is divided into Centre and East Moriches. The Hotel Brooklyn and the Moriches Inn are the leading hotels here. They are attractive modern structures, well appointed, and enjoy a fine patronage. Moriches, like almost all the places along Moriches Bay and the Great South Bay, of which the former

HOTEL BROOKLYN, CENTRE MORICHES

49

is an extension, affords the opportunity of either still-water
bathing, where the children may enjoy themselves to the fullest
extent with absolute safety, or, by a short sail across the bay,
of surf bathing of the finest kind.

Moriches has always enjoyed the greatest popularity, and
is one of the most important resorts on Long Island. Its
summer population is composed of a class of people who seek
the wholesome enjoyments of out-of-door life rather than the
attractions of society, and as a consequence the day is largely
given over to sailing, bathing, rowing, and sports on land.
Hundreds of families from New York and Brooklyn make this
place their summer home, and, knowing its charms, would
not for a moment entertain an idea of going anywhere else.
No more ideal spot could be found for those who love the
water. Moriches Bay is practically land-locked, and perfectly
safe for sailing or rowing at all times. There is neither danger
of sudden squalls nor rough water. Along the beach of the
bay the still-water bathing is delightful, and, as at the other
nearby places, a short sail takes those who wish a plunge in the
surf over to the outlying island, where the ocean breaks upon

one of the finest beaches in America. There are a great
number of attractive boarding-houses in Moriches, where accommodations from the most modest to the most pretentious

THE MORICHES INN

kind may be had. Moriches is one of the most popular summering places on Long Island.

Eastport is not quite so near the bay as either of its
neighbors, Moriches or Speonk. It commands a beautiful
view, however, of not only the bay, with the deep, blue ocean

THE LONG ISLAND COUNTRY CLUBHOUSE, EASTPORT

51

beyond, but of the surrounding country. It is located on elevated ground in a section full of agricultural possibilities, where already the hand of the modern scientific farmer is evident in the many improved country places. The Long Island Country Club has established its new and beautiful home here, at the edge of one of the several lakes which add to the beauty and variety of the country.

Speonk takes on during the season, when the summer population, which returns to it each year, is present, the activity of quite a town. It has a colony of attractive cottages, a Presbyterian church, and a number of delightful features.

With the picturesque village of Westhampton, the first of the famous group of summer resorts known familiarly as "The Hamptons" begins. This is the first of the places to be reached on Long Island east of Far Rockaway and Long Beach where the ocean, with its magnificent surf, may be reached by road instead of by sail across the intervening bay. The town of Westhampton is partly concealed from view at the railroad station by heavy woods, and the traveler passing through upon the train gets but a suggestion of its beauty. The water is reached by a handsome broad road, from which laterals lead both east and west. The golf links are good and admirably laid out, the surrounding country affording ample space for this popular pastime. There are many attractive homes bordering on them occupied by summer residents. One of the historic places here is that which was formerly the home of General John A. Dix, who gave the patriotic order that "If any man attempts to haul down the American flag, shoot him on the spot!" The ancestral place is now the summer home of the General's son, Rev. Dr. Morgan Dix.

Quogue, a well-known seat of summer society, is located upon the first undulations, which find their greatest altitude in the Shinnecock Hills. It is a delightful country, with wide stretches of open space, and so near the ocean that bathing is easily the predominating enjoyment of the summer season. Among the traditions to which Quogue clings tenaciously is that De Witt Clinton and Daniel Webster used to spend their vacation days here, enjoying in the fullest degree the bathing and the fishing, with the attendant shore dinner. Hence it comes that fish dinners are in these modern days the popular thing at this charming little place by the sea.

A SOUTH SHORE LIFE-SAVING STATION

There are a large number of fine boarding-houses and small hotels at Quogue, at which excellent board may be secured. It is a characteristic feature of this delightful place that those who have ever spent a summer here return on succeeding seasons. There are a number of well-stocked stores, and all of the best facilities for sailing, fishing, and bathing. The golf links are fast obtaining an enviable reputation. Nature has been liberal if not prolific in its distribution hereabouts of such land as is particularly adapted to this popular recreation.

Good Ground is situated almost midway between Quogue on the west and Shinnecock Hills on the east, and, from its rather elevated location, commands a beautiful view of the ocean and of Shinnecock Bay—which lies to the east of Moriches Bay, and forms a part of the chain of inland waters between the ocean and the attractive main shore of Long Island. There are in the town and its immediate vicinity a number of excellent boarding places.

Beyond Good Ground the engine tells by its puffing that it has reached the grade leading up to and among the Shinnecock Hills. Here is where the modern marine artist has erected his temple and brought his palette, for there are few spots anywhere which offer more tempting inspirations for the brush or pencil. To the north the view extends over the beautiful and sparkling Peconic Bay, which has split the island

53

at its eastern end into two portions. To the south is the peaceful Shinnecock Bay, and beyond it, and separated from it by the low-lying bar, so narrow as to be hardly visible, is the mighty ocean. Connecting the waters of Peconic and Shinnecock bays is a canal, originally cut through the sand hills by the Indians more than two centuries ago. New York State during recent years has made this canal navigable for small boats. Upon the shore of the bay is an old inn of English pattern and furnishing, where comfortable accomodations may be had. Near it is a tavern of ancient times but modern comforts, which has been a popular abiding place for a hundred years. There are growing in front of it two immense willows, grown from slips brought from St. Helena, and a notable exterior decoration is a colossal wooden statue of Hercules, the weather-worn figurehead of the famous old United States warship "Ohio."

In the cemetery of a quaint little church near by, in which he preached, is the grave of the last of the Indian missionaries, Rev. Paul Cuffee, and not far away are the ruins of an old fort.

Up to a comparatively few years ago the Shinnecock Hills had not felt the touch of modern development, and reposed quietly and peacefully in the glories of their past. A company of enterprising gentlemen rediscovered them, and, instantly recognizing the charm of their location and the healthfulness of such a spot, almost surrounded as it is by water, they purchased large areas of property and began to systematically develop and improve them. To-day there are many beautiful villas, and each season there gathers here a congenial coterie of summer visitors who find perpetual pleasure in the rare opportunities the place affords for all kinds of out-of-door life. Golf is a popular pastime, and the links are excellent.

The railroad, after passing through the hills, descends again into the gentler scenery, where the fields are broad and fertile. The impression that the region has long been tilled is not belied by its history, for it was first settled in 1640, and Job's Lane, still an avenue of travel, was opened in 1663. A number of the houses were built more than two centuries ago.

Southampton bears upon its face so unmistakably the stamp of social approval that the most hurried glance shows that its claim to be one of the most popular and at the same time delightful resorts upon Long Island is well founded.

54

OLD WINDMILLS IN THE EAST END OF LONG ISLAND

It is a town of villas and charming cottages, and its sparkling little lake is surrounded by these homes of wealth and
culture, which compare most favorably in architectural beauty
with those at any resort in America. The price of ground is
as metropolitan as the general atmosphere of the place, and as
a location for people of social instincts and wealth it is ideal.
Among its notable features is the commodious home of the
Hampton Club. There are at Southampton a large number of
comfortable boarding-houses, where those who do not possess
their own villas may enjoy the summer life to the fullest de-

THE LIBRARY AT SOUTHAMPTON

gree. The town is not without its old-time heroes, for it was a
Southampton whaler, Mercator Cooper, who, by returning
a crew of shipwrecked Japanese sailors to their native home,
first invited the friendship of Japan, and made it the easier
for Commodore Perry to succeed in opening the ports of that
country to American shipping. Many of the old sailors who
were formerly engaged in whaling still live in Southampton,
and are ready to serve the visitors in their sailing and fishing
excursions.

MECOX INN, WATER MILL

Beyond Southampton, and the only place between it and Bridgehampton, is the quiet little resort of Water Mill, situated close to an arm of Mecox Bay, and offering, because of its ideal location, many inducements to the summer home-seeker and artist.

On high land overlooking Mecox Bay and the ocean is "The Mecox Inn at Watermill," a new and well-equipped hotel, accommodating 100 guests. It is modern in every respect, fitted throughout with gas and electric bells, and the rooms are large with commodious closets. The table and service are first-class in every respect.

Bridgehampton is a vigorous old-time village, with white churches, vine-embowered cottages, and an ancient windmill, one of a large number of similar constructions which are still "attending to business at the old stand" on the eastern end of Long Island. Its population is busily engaged in its farming and fishing, but the summer residents will find a cordial welcome awaiting them, and most excellent accommodations in the several hotels and comfortable houses which are open for their reception. There is here a good public library and a number of churches.

At Bridgehampton the south shore line of the railroad forms a Y, one line turning almost due north and terminating at Sag Harbor on Peconic Bay, and the other continuing east to Montauk almost at the tip end of the island.

Sag Harbor is going down in American maritime history along with Nantucket and Portsmouth, for with them it divided honors during the years when whaling was one of the foremost of our coast industries. In appearance it is the Nantucket of Long Island, and clings tenaciously to the quaint old customs and habits of a century ago, when, as marvelous

57

A LONG ISLAND DUCK FARM

as the statement may seem, the tonnage of its harbor was as great as that of New York, and its income from the whale fishery alone was more than a million dollars a year. Its harbor used to be filled with sailing vessels of the staunchest type, and its village life gay with the coming and going of hardy seafaring men. It is claimed that its streets, like some of those of Boston, are dignified cowpaths, which wander here and there regardless of surveyor's lines. The main thoroughfare has, however, made strenuous efforts to be respectably straight, and is lined with good shops and hotels. The little town has assumed, despite its antiquity, considerable of that which is modern, and has gas, water-works, attractive churches, and excellent schools, including a convent school of more than local fame. Sag Harbor is a place of considerable importance in the manufacturing line, one of the largest watch-case factories in America being located here. It was here that the magnificent silver service presented to the U. S. cruiser "Brooklyn" was made.

A hunting and fishing club has established itself upon the neighboring shores of Peconic Bay, and here and there are numerous modern summer homes, with delightful surroundings of lawn and shade. Taken in its entirety, Sag Harbor offers as many and as varied attractions as any place to be named within equal distance of New York.

THE MAIDSTONE CLUBHOUSE AT EASTHAMPTON

Continuing east from Bridgehampton, Wainscott station is reached, which is a mile and a half from the ancient hamlet of that name. Whether its natives are more fishermen than farmers is questionable; but they certainly rival the Amagansett folk, eastward, in their love of whale catching. Some of them have descended from the thirty-five original purchasers of Easthampton township in 1649, and still live upon the land of their forefathers. Wainscott Pond (a pickerel pond of much local repute) and Georgica Lake, which is just eastward, are certainly the most picturesque of Long Island ponds, and next to Mecox, the largest. The facilities afforded here for

THE CLINTON ACADEMY AT EASTHAMPTON

sailing and fresh-water bathing, and the proximity of the
ocean, which is separated from the lake only by a strip of
sandy beach one-half mile long and a biscuit-toss in width,
give it every advantage of location. There is perfect freedom
from irksome conventionalities and causes of ill-health. Its
excellent facilities for tennis, golf, and other forms of sport
make this one of the most delightful spots on Long Island.

IN BEAUTIFUL EASTHAMPTON

There are a half-score or more of picturesque cottages located
in the most attractive places and occupied during the summer
season by their owners, who are among the best known of
New York and Brooklyn's professional and business men.

Every ear in Christendom has heard the tender strains of
"Home, Sweet Home," but there are comparatively few who
know that its author, John Howard Payne, was born in this

quiet little village of Easthampton. It was back to this
peaceful, beautiful town that the thought of the wandering
poet was ever turning, and it was a quaint old house, still
standing, that became the theme of his world-circling song.
To the sight-seeing tourist or the sojourner in Easthampton,
this plain abode, "ever so humble," is one of the chief sights
of interest. Idealized by a poet's fancy, the bareness of the
faded reality cannot wholly dispel the glamour of sentiment
surrounding this weather-beaten dwelling. To myriads of the
sons of men in every land and of every tongue, it has stood
for home. It was in Easthampton, too, that Lyman Beecher
long resided. Among others whose home or birthplace it has
been are Lion Gardiner, one of the first settlers, whose tomb
is surmounted by a knight in armor recumbent; John Alex-
ander Tyler, Roscoe Conkling, Rev. T. DeWitt Talmage, and
Thomas Moran, the painter of Western scenery.

The main street of the town, lined with splendid old trees,
is over one hundred and thirty feet wide, and the beach, fac-
ing the open sea, is one of the finest on the Atlantic coast. It
was here, so the legend runs, that Europeans landed and re-
connoitered long before the Pilgrim feet touched Plymouth
Rock; and the actual settlement was one of the earliest in this
region. Here are found to-day many picturesque legacies of

THE OLD WINDMILL, EASTHAMPTON

61

MAIN STREET, EASTHAMPTON

this old time. Among them are three Dutch windmills, whose quaint arms give to the landscape a touch of Holland; a sunken pool, where the will-o'-the-wisp is said to still have its haunt; an old burying-ground, under whose hoary stones the "fathers of the hamlet sleep;" and an ancient seat of learning, Clinton Academy, through whose gambrel-roof dormer windows peer curiously. But Easthampton, like many places of historic interest, lives not so much in the past as in the present day. It is the delightful home town of a refined society, and the invigorating pleasures it offers for summer residence make it a haven for those seeking escape from the city's heat and stress. There have been built in recent years many handsome summer homes at Easthampton, and each year sees the building of a number of modern country cottages. Golf playing has here become very popular, and at no point on Long Island are the natural facilities more pronounced than at Easthampton. With the ever-cooling breezes from the ocean on one hand and the undulating country on the other, this royal sport is greatly enjoyed. The Maidstone Clubhouse is a model of arrangement and convenience.

THE PRINCIPAL STREET OF EASTHAMPTON

THE HOWARD PAYNE HOUSE, EASTHAMPTON

The pretty village of Amagansett lies a little to the east, at a point where the most picturesque section of the island really begins. It is surrounded by a rich farming region, and itself embodies the placid spirit of its pastoral environs.

Continuing east, the terminus of the railway is reached at Montauk, on the waters of Fort Pond Bay. Beyond the hamlet is the long, open peninsula of Montauk Point, rising to a height above the sea of from fifty to one hundred feet. Its surface is rolling, and in the hollows are many quiet ponds on whose bosoms lily-pads float. Toward the ocean the hills become cliffs of gravel, often from ninety to a hundred feet in height, rising straight up from the sea. On this steep shore many a good ship has gone down, notwithstanding the warnings that gleam from the lighthouse; but there has been only a small loss of life, owing to the efficiency of the life-saving station located here. Until a few years ago there were but three houses on the long twenty-mile stretch of the Point, and before many seasons have passed it will doubtless be well settled. Already a village has been located far out on the Point, where the breezes blow up fresh from the sea. The dwellers in it can sail in fact or in fancy without touching land until the shores of Europe are reached. The sand dunes, the hills, the roving cattle, the unending ocean—there is a tonic in it all, exhilarating alike to mind and body. Looking out over the waters, one sees the lands beyond them, rich in the lore of the ages. Rolling behind are the land waves of the undulating Point, lonely, dreamy. One seems to be at a joining, in some mystical union, of the land and the sea; the ethereal ocean stretches above, flecked with island clouds; the air is a blending of salt and balm, both bracing and soothing; it is in such a setting of sea and sky, land and breeze, that those find them-

MONTAUK LIGHT

EXTREME END OF LONG ISLAND AT MONTAUK POINT

selves who journey for their summer outing to Montauk Point, where Long Island plunges into the Atlantic.

Montauk—famous Montauk—a haven of rest and recuperation for the noble of the land! After the close of the late war the army surgeons selected Montauk from all the magnificent coast line of America as the ideal camping-ground upon which to build up our overtaxed and worn-out warriors. Here in less than thirty days was raised a camp of thirty thousand soldiers, including several regiments of cavalry, accompanied by their horses and implements of war. The spacious Fort Pond Bay at Montauk suddenly became the scene of the greatest activity; for in place of fishing boats, floating or drifting, with their lazy sails floating out to catch the breeze, the bay was filled quickly with United States war vessels flying the Stars and Stripes, and transports hurrying from Cuba with their precious cargoes of invalids; all energy, all rush, all hurry to only get ashore to the Mecca of rest, the land of promise—beautiful Montauk.

At the extreme end of the island stands the tall, white tower of the Montauk Point Lighthouse. Its powerful Fresnel light,

OFF MONTAUK

a gift of the French government, can throw its rays twenty miles out to sea on the darkest nights.

Hovering over this lonely coast are many legends of Indian and pirate. Of course, the famous Captain Kidd, "as he sailed," couldn't avoid stopping on Montauk, and the bags of treasure, captured on the Spanish Main, which he is supposed to have sunk in one of the patches of water, have given to it the name of Money Pond. It was here on the Point that the

THE INN AT MONTAUK

famous old chief of the Montauks, Wyandance, had the seat
of his aboriginal government. There is more than legend in
support of this, as the remains of his settlement may still be
seen. The Montauks were firm friends of the whites, especially of Lion Gardiner, in whom they had steadfast confi-
dence. Their loyal good-will was a great boon to the early
settlers, a fact which may have had something to do in the
handing down of traditions attributing to the Indians marvelous power over the genii of the air and water.

It is surely no idle fancy to say that such abundance of
tradition, always an alluring field of exploration, such wealth
of scenery and such abounding opportunities to have rest and
recreation, now that the Long Island Railroad has made them
accessible, will make of Montauk Point summer resorts. For
building sites these hills, looking in each direction on the
ocean, are unsurpassed. They command not merely view, but
health, for the air has the vim of the sea's salt in it, the water
is cool and pure, and the drainage is perfect. Tucked in here
and there under the hills are safe harbors for all manner of
pleasure craft. Indeed, now that distance has been changed
by the railroad from many miles to a few hours, there is nothing
lacking at Montauk to make of it one of the great resorts of
the Atlantic coast. That is, nothing is lacking which man,
drawn to the Point by its manifold advantages, will not very
shortly supply. Hotels and cottages are following fast in the
track of the railroad, and they will have to multiply themselves
to keep pace with the increasing population. The new Montauk Inn affords ample accommodation for transient guests.

67

SUBURBAN TOWNS

INCE January 1, 1898, a considerable portion of Greater New York, both as regards population and territory, has been on Long Island. It has come about, therefore, that many towns which have hitherto been suburbs are now included in the greater city. But this fact has not deprived them of their rural beauties. They still dot the green stretches of Long Island, an air of peaceful comfort and domesticity investing them. Their inhabitants have the consciousness of dwelling in the city while enjoying country life.

Passing through the Boroughs of Brooklyn and Queens on the Long Island Railroad, one soon reaches Morris Park and Richmond Hill, on the way to Jamaica. These towns are especially adapted for the homes of those whose means are moderate, and whose families require room to grow in. Schools are excellent, and the social life wholesome. These advantages are combined with accessibility to one's place of business.

STATE NORMAL SCHOOL, JAMAICA

68

SOME OF THE LONG ISLAND RAILROAD STATIONS

Morris Park is a pretty place, in which the price of lots is still reasonable. Richmond Hill, just beyond, is somewhat older, and its broad streets, well-kept lawns, and comfortable homes unite in giving a most favorable impression to even a casual visitor. These charms are more manifest the longer one tarries, and they have bound a growing population to the pleasant town in most loyal fealty. The location is sufficiently elevated to give excellent drainage and a fine view of the surrounding country. Richmond Hill has superb golf links, and the game is exceedingly popular and largely played here. A hurried glance at these charming hamlets, even from a car window, discovers abundant reasons for their rapid growth.

Jamaica, settled in 1656, is a happy blending of the old and new. With many interesting survivals of its early days, it possesses an old-time background, which throws into strong relief such modern conveniences as electric lights, gas, local surface cars, and very frequent train service. The town's dominant note is stability. Without lacking in progress, it still appears settled and finished. Jamaica is the railroad centre of Long Island. It is the hub through which lines radiate from Brooklyn and from Long Island City to the main and southern divisions, and to Oyster Bay, Port Jefferson, Greenport and Sag Harbor, and Montauk. About it are the material evidences of the railroad centre, such as shops, sheds, and the like. The town is rapidly increasing in population, having now over 7,000 inhabitants. That ephemeral prominence long since gave way to the substantial prosperity of this era of homes and railroads.

Going on east of Jamaica, one comes to the pretty town of Hollis. Its pleasant dwellings are surrounded by generous yards, gay with the bloom of many flowers. There is a satisfactory variety in the architecture, the Queen Anne style sharing honors with the Colonial and the modern. The founders of the town were far-sighted enough to plant many trees, which have now reached a stalwart size, giving to the broad driveways a grateful shade. From the ridge to the north of Hollis a splendid view is afforded, embracing sea and land, farm and city, the hills of Jersey far away touching the sky on the western horizon.

Interstate Park is the last addition to the attractions of the Long Island Railroad. The recent National shooting

A FAVORITE ROAD ON THE NORTH SIDE

contests were held here. Owing to its natural advantages for matches, it has attracted within its borders the most enthusiastic gunners of the country. At the recent International contest gunners from California, Texas, Mexico and Canada assembled here to struggle for the great continental trophy—the championship of the continent.

During these contests, in addition to the regular schedule, special trains are run to and from New York and Brooklyn.

A suitable clubhouse is in course of construction, and when completed will be a rendezvous of the champion gunners of the continent.

ON THE CREEDMOOR RIFLE RANGE

Built on a rolling plain, a little farther on, is Queens, named for the county in which it is situated. It is a quiet, home-like village, whose old church, standing among tall cedars, with the encircling fields, combines to produce the effect of a quaint English hamlet. The good air here gives a keen edge to one's appetite, and the charming environs offer constant invitations to trips afoot or awheel. Long hills stretch across the north, forming the backbone of the island. Spreading at their feet toward the sea is a wide plain. There is a look half suggesting Holland in much of the landscape. There are gardens, the grazing cattle and the windmills. At Creedmoor, to the north, are the rifle ranges where the great international competitions are held. The name of the town is coupled with rifle records the world over.

From rifles one shifts to roses in the next village, Floral Park, which is known far and near for the seeds and flowers that go from it. It was given new life by John Lewis Childs when he located his nurseries and greenhouses here. So successful has been the raising of seeds that the business has spread over the town to the exclusion of nearly all other enterprises. Every condition of soil and climate favors, and there seems to be no good reason why the raising of flowers, as well as seeds, cannot be carried on to the point where the city's great demand can be almost wholly supplied. The little park whence the town gets its name, reached just before the station, is a thing of beauty when all abloom during the summer. From an observatory in it one can look over this great seed and flower farm, for such it is, and see the fine houses and cottages that dot it.

The fertile township of Hempstead, large enough for a county, begins here with the plains of Garden City. This town is the See city of the Diocese of Long Island, and was founded by the late A. T. Stewart. It is a religious, educational, and social centre. Grouped about the beautiful Cathedral are a number of schools, including the famous St. Paul's school for boys, endowed and erected by Mrs. A. T. Stewart, as a memorial to her husband. It is a splendid building, and from it through the trees the tall spire of the Cathedral is seen, exquisite in its Gothic beauty. Here is also located St. Mary's school for young ladies. It was A. T. Stewart's design in laying out the town to make of it a dwelling place for those of moderate means. This has been considerably departed from, owing to the attractions of the town

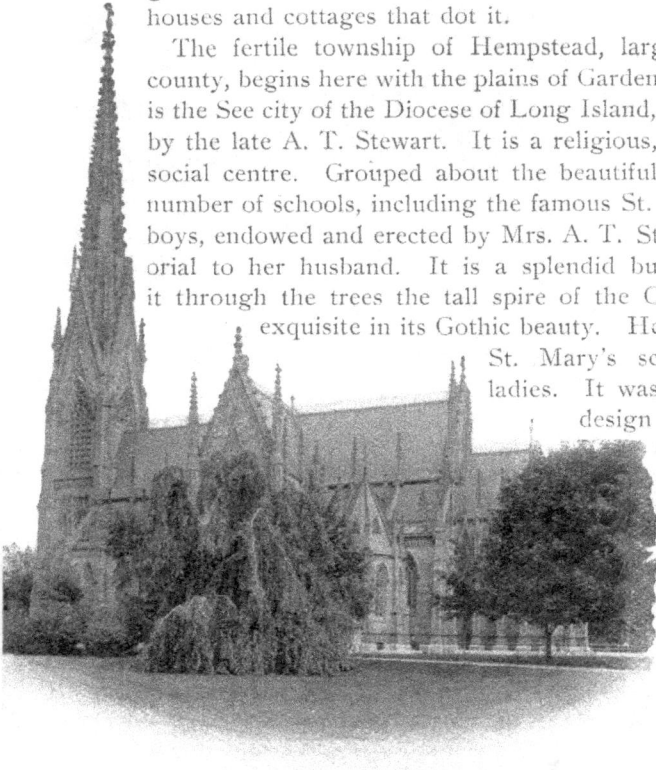

THE CATHEDRAL AT GARDEN CITY

having drawn to it many people of wealth, whose homes make a rich setting for the religious and educational institutions of which it is the seat. The Cathedral is the Stewart family mausoleum. Its ecclesiastical importance, together with the impressive beauty of its service and music, draw to it worshippers from a large area, as far even as New York and Brooklyn. The beautiful hotel, which was formerly the social centre of Garden City, was destroyed by fire, but a new structure is rising in its stead which will have all the attractiveness of the old and many modern features. Garden

THE INTERIOR OF THE GARDEN CITY CATHEDRAL

City, among other attractions, is the home of the Carteret Gun Club, a popular social, sportsmen's association.

To one who may not have the good fortune to dwell amid these surroundings, the Garden City Golf Club stands to-day in the front rank of associations. Neither money nor time is spared to maintain the high standard attained. Special trains are run upon the Long Island road from New York and Brooklyn to accommodate the players.

The old and the new are strikingly united in Hempstead, a mile or so farther on. Its history dates back to the Revolution and beyond, for the Episcopal Church possesses a communion service which was presented to it by Queen Anne. During the Revolution the red-coats occupied the town, and the hotel where Washington stayed, the old Town Hall, and some of the first houses are still standing. The very button-ball trees shading its pleasant streets are one hundred and fifty years old.

But the march of modern improvement has not passed old Hempstead by. It possesses the usual comforts of a latter-day town, and one can see the historic houses by brilliant electric lights from the smoothest of macadamized roadways. The

VIEWS IN GARDEN CITY

society is of the best, and many fine homes have b e e n erected here by well-known New Yorkers of wealth. Near by are the Meadowbrook and Farm Kennel Clubs. Their meets and hunts are celebrated among the gentlemen sportsmen of the entire continent.

The first railroad on the island ran to Hempstead sixty years ago, and eight years later the line was extended to Greenport. The main line and southern division of the Long Island road are joined by a line running from Garden City to Valley Stream, on which are located West Hempstead, Hempstead Gardens, and Norwood.

75

POLO AT MEADOWBROOK

At the outbreak of the late war, and about two miles north-ward from Hempstead, was established the immense Camp Black, so named in honor of the Governor of the State. Here, in training, were several thousand men—infantry, artillery, and cavalry.

The location upon which Camp Black was established was selected at the commencement of the war (as was Camp Wikoff at Montauk at the cessation of hostilities) because of its splendid location, its high and dry lands and undulating surface.

It would be very difficult to find a greater tribute to the general and specific healthfulness of Long Island than that paid by the United States Government in the selecting of both ends of the island for the mobilization and recuperation of her troops.

MEADOWBROOK CLUB RETURNING FROM THE HUNT

THE CENTRAL SECTION

T HE central section of Long Island is still within the zone of accessibility to the city. While the time required to reach it is, of course, longer than with the towns grouped about Jamaica, it is not long enough by any means to serve as a bar to this region's becoming a popular place of suburban residence. Its advantages of open country and pure air have already won as permanent residents many who do business in New York and Brooklyn. As the area of crowded population is inevitably extended farther into the island, these advantages will be more fully appreciated.

Hyde Park, on the main line, east of Jamaica, is a growing town of well-built modern houses, with fertile stretches of farm land surrounding it.

Mineola, a little further on, the county seat of the new Nassua county, is especially noted for its agricultural fairs, held every autumn. At these there is always a fine show of the rich bounties of Nassau County and Queens Borough farms and much fine-blooded stock. It is the country supporting this fair that long ago gave Long Island a good name for its farm products.

LONG ISLAND PRODUCTS

77

In the slightly rolling region beyond is the pleasant little town of Westbury, known as the home of many prominent New Yorkers. On the edge of the hills are a number of handsome homes and clubhouses. The lands about are good to till, to tramp over, or just to own for the satisfaction that comes through a constant increase in value. The rolling, hilly nature of the land hereabouts has made Westbury very popular as a golfing centre.

Hicksville has been worked over by the spirit of change and improvement. Its factories have been enlarged in number and output. Their prosperity has been reflected in many new cottages built for their workmen. There is a thriving aspect about the town, and one has a feeling of solid comfort in looking down the shady vista of its wide, clean main street.

LAKE AND WOODLAND

Where the air smells sweet from the fragrance of a young pine wood, you come upon Central Park. Though but a little town, it has a bright, clean look, and its roads, leading out over leagues of level farm land, are a joy to ride upon.

Farmingdale, less than thirty miles from Broadway, New York City, enjoys a most charming situation. With high hills on the north, churches, public schools, School of Technology, brick yards and factories, it has a pleasant and healthful surrounding, with fine macadamized drives, and is one of the growing villages. Farther on are the Comac Hills, among which is West Deer Park. Here the woods thicken and the trees grow taller. Near by are some springs which were formerly considered of medicinal value. Systematic development of large areas of its land is being carried on by a company that is alert to the possibilities of the place.

Brentwood brings one farther within the pine belt. It is an excellent health resort. The fresh sea breezes passing over the conifers absorb an elixir that brightens and invigorates.

The woods are interspersed with farms, gardens, and nurseries. In the town is located an academy for young ladies, conducted by the Sisters of St. Joseph.

Central Islip is also in the pine belt. The prevailing conditions—pure air, clear water and abundance of ozone, all in the midst of a great pine belt, make this district a most favorable place for residence. Central Islip, with its attractive homes, good schools and fine churches, gives evidence of the high character of its inhabitants.

Passing a bit of fenland, an unusual thing to see in this part of Long Island, one comes to the village of the pretty Indian name, Ronkonkoma. It is scattered over a long stretch. largely of farms, reaching to Holtsville, a place partly owned by the Waverly Gun Club. The farms here are marked by the idyllic simplicity of the long ago. Near the doors of little red or white houses, "iron-bound buckets hang in the well."

THE EAST SHORE OF LAKE RONKONKOMA

LAKE FRONT HOTEL, RONKONKOMA

One of the real beauty spots of Long Island is Lake Ronkonkoma, a little way north of the village of the same name. The sheen of its limpid surface sparkles like the eyes of an Indian maiden. Fed by springs at the bottom, its waters are as pure as they are clear. The lake is about three miles around, and its shores form the shape of a pear. In places it is over sixty feet deep. As a shady fringe around it are many trees, and clustered about are a number of cottages. Along the beach of white sand a road runs, and the view from it over the crystal face of the lake is beautiful. This is the largest and finest body of fresh water on Long Island. It is fifty-five feet above sea level.

Through some mystery of nature it has periods of ebb and flood, but these are not coincident with the tides or by any possibility connected with them. In the darkling depths, bass, catfish, and perch disport themselves. Floating now and again over its bosom, as if calling its Indian name, are the sounds of bells from St. Mary's-by-the-Lake, and from other steeples. A legend has it that a phantom canoe now and again glides noiselessly over the waters bearing an Indian girl, love-lorn, and in search of the young brave to whom she has given her heart. With the dawn her birch-bark boat skims away into the ether and the sun looks down into the mirror face of Ronkonkoma.

Among wide stretches of plain and forest beyond the lake is the town of Medford. Any one longing for "a lodge in some vast wilderness" can find it in this region. The town with its first syllable indicating midway, is very nearly at the middle point of the island, east and west.

One of the queerest names to be found, Yaphank, is the bit of nomenclature to which the next town answers from out its setting of green fields and fine old woods. It is such a setting and such an atmosphere as an artist will travel far to find.

Great fens lie round about Manor, at which point the main and south lines of the Long Island Railroad connect, and the

CRANBERRY PICKING ON LONG ISLAND

Peconic River flows near by on its eastward course toward Great Peconic Bay. There are new shops and an old tavern in the town.

Farms and forest contend for supremacy at Calverton, which is also near the river. Strawberries, cauliflower, and potatoes are raised here. Cranberries were also recently introduced in the territory lying between here and Riverhead. The natural facilities are so excellent for the propagation of this delicious berry that the celebrated Cape Cod berry no longer holds pre-eminence, excepting in quantity. No finer cranberry is produced in the markets of the United States than those grown in the neighborhood of Calverton and Riverhead. The element

81

of picturesqueness is contributed by the hilly surface and the woods, where dark green pines and silvery white-stemmed birches mingle.

Riverhead contains about three thousand people, a population much augmented during a part of the year by the summer contingent. It is a pleasant, thrifty place. Views from high places about Riverhead embrace not alone the undulating country, but the bright waters of the Atlantic in one direction about an hour's drive from town, and Peconic Bay in another. The bay and the river are navigable up to this

MAIN STREET, RIVERHEAD

point for small craft. Shops, lumber yards, mills, and a cigar factory provide business. Riverhead has a watering place, too—at Flanders, about two miles away. Fishing, shooting, boating and bathing are greatly enjoyed. There is also a body of water near the town with the romantic name of Wildwood Lake.

ALONG PECONIC BAY

LONG the always beautiful and picturesque Peconic Bay are a number of towns and villages, where the fine climate, good roads, and general attractions are making them prime favorites with summer visitors. The bay itself is a beautiful body of salt water, on whose placid bosom all manner of pleasure craft can be seen during the warm months, bearing happy groups of care-free folk. They sail or row over the blue waters in land-locked security from the rollers of the open sea. If they wish to take a dip, good beaches offer the alluring opportunity.

On the north side of the bay, after leaving Riverhead, one soon comes to the town of Aquebogue, a name admirably descriptive, for water and bog make up the bay-front side. The

ON PECONIC BAY

83

Saxon half of the name and the sedgy flats about the town sug-
gest the marshes of Runnymede, where the barons wrested the
Magna Charta from King John.

The land rises as one reaches Jamesport, and here are hills
crowned with old churches and pleasant homes. This town has
become so popular for a summer holiday that the difficulty frequently met with is getting accommodations, a fact that has
served as a stimulus in the erection of many cottages.

Laurel is a pretty village, "at peace with all the world."
Contentment exhales from it as a fragrance, and it always has
a colony of summer residents.

MATTITUCK CREEK

A little way on down the narrow Italy-shaped peninsula
into which the north side of Long Island is here tapering is
the pretty village of Mattituck. Both to the north and to the
south it has fine water advantages. Having comforable and
hospitable farmhouses for the entertainment of visitors, it has
won deserved repute as a place of summer outing. One of the

diversions of those sojourning here is found in a little creek flowing toward the Sound and abounding in crabs.

"Just sneeze and you pronounce it." That is a remark the writer overheard as descriptive of the name Cutchogue. But this description is suggestive in ways other than phonetically. A sneeze is apt to result from too much oxygen, and in the air that blows fresh from the water over sightly Cutchogue, and its neighbor, New Suffolk, oxygen is abundant. Good air and a fine view are not the only advantages of this pleasing resort. It has one of the best roads in America, the long, straight highway leading from Riverhead to Orient. But good roads on Long Island, it should be said, are the rule

SUMMER CAMP ON PECONIC BAY

rather than the exception. Every natural advantage in surface and soil helps their construction and maintenance. The drainage is good, the grades seldom steep, and there is plenty of land to give the roads needed width. As a result these highways between verdant stretches of farm land, in the shade of noble trees, by the shores of shining lakes, and in sight often of the mighty sea, offer a perpetual invitation to walking, cycling, and driving.

One's first impression of Peconic, formed from a glance down its broad, shaded street, is favorable, and closer acquaintance with the old town confirms this impression. Southold, a few miles east, lays claim to antiquity in its name, and points to the fact proudly that its first settlers secured a

concession from the Indians and formed a church as early
as 1640. There is a contention between Southold and Southampton, across the bay, as to which is the older. In August,
1890, Southold celebrated, with much ceremony, the two hundred and fiftieth anniversary of its founding. The town has a
centre where the stores, schools, and churches are grouped,
and about it the houses are scattered widely. Whichever
way the wind may blow the old place is fanned by a sea breeze.
In this fact summer antiquarians profess to have found a reason for the great age of some of the inhabitants, a few of
whom, it is claimed, antedate the founding of the place.

Journeying to the very end of the main line of the Long
Island Railroad one reaches the progressive and interesting
town of Greenport. It has over 3,000 inhabitants, and is both
a resort and an important business centre. Small steamers
ply between Sag Harbor, Greenport and New London, Conn.
Within the safe haven of its harbor a mighty fleet could find
anchorage. Boating, sailing, fishing, and shooting are excellent, and many pleasant trips can be made awheel, afloat,
or afoot. The view one gets from a bluff north of the town

THE SOUND SHORE NEAR GREENPORT

86

VIEWS IN AND ABOUT SOUTHOLD

MARION LAKE, EAST MARION

is expansive and exhilarating. Dancing in the sunlight are the waters of the Sound stretching away to the green shores of Connecticut; to the south lies Peconic Bay, a glittering sapphire set between the green heights of Shelter Island and the trees of Greenport, with spire and roof peering through them; to east and west the eye travels over water to the far horizon.

This north prong of Long Island pushes on from Greenport, beyond the pretty villages of East Marion and Orient, always attractive to summer visitors, to its end at Orient Point. Here the land, which has been gradually becoming narrower, dips into the sea.

THE LAKE AT EAST MARION

SHELTER ISLAND

LOATING on the land-locked waters between Gardiner's Bay and Peconic Bay, opposite Greenport, is Shelter Island. From the time of the Indian up to the present it has fulfilled its name. In the red man's quaint phrase, it was "the island sheltered by islands," and he knew that if he could get his canoe within any of the harbors along its coast he would be safe. But the island did not get its name from the Indian's phrase, but from the fact that some Quakers, exiled by the Puritans, and wandering, heart-sick and weary, in search of a refuge, here found a shelter, under the protecting arm of the tolerant Nathaniel Sylvester. To these Quakers it was a "rock in a weary land, and a shelter in the time of storm"; and in gratitude for the haven they bequeathed to it the name of Shelter. Sylvester was engaged in the sugar trade in the West Indies when he acted the part of patron to the friendless Friends, and permitted their founder, George Fox, to preach from the front steps of his manor-house. This structure, the centre of much gaiety and hospitality, was built of bricks brought over from Holland, with queer biblical tiles for the chimneys, and with windows and doors from England or Barbadoes. The prim floral denizens of the old-fashioned garden were immigrants, too, and to this day a flourishing boxtree and a hawthorn hedge attest the loving care of the first lords of the manor. The surrounding woods were cut away to furnish timber for hogsheads used in the sugar trade. The present manor-house, almost on the site of the original one, belongs to a later day, yet it is over a hundred years old. It was the summer residence of the late Professor Hosford, of Harvard, and with his co-operation a monument was erected commemorating the landing of those early Quakers. These were not the only exiles to whom Sylvester extended a brotherly hand. When the uncompromising Puritans had imprisoned,

A VIEW OF THE HARBOR FROM SHELTER ISLAND

PECONIC BAY FROM SHELTER ISLAND

whipped, and banished Lawrence and Cassandra Southwick from Boston because of their faith, these unfortunates also found a refuge in Shelter Island, where they passed the rest of their lives with the kindly inhabitants. Shelter Island to-day maintains its right to the ancient name, though in a different, end-of-the-century way. Now it is the haven of many harassed, toil-driven, heat-oppressed business men. Here is found in hotel or cottage a place of comfort or rest. The irregular shore, diversified surfaces, and fine beaches of the island help make it attractive. Boating and bathing are enjoyed. The great Manhanset Hotel affords accommodations for six hundred people, and has a splendid frontage of seven hundred and twenty-five feet on the water. Handsome and well appointed, it is justly popular. The Shelter Island Yacht Club and the New York Yacht Club each has its own house there. The Prospect House is one of the best-known and best-liked hotels in this region, and is situated at Shelter Island Heights. Here the Shelter Island Association, organized to build cottages and improve the real estate of the Heights, has obtained a supply of pure spring water for the houses, laid out roads and paths, and established restrictions for the community's well-being. The popular Shelter Island

Golf Links are located here. The game is largely played, and during the whole season presents probably more animation and enthusiasm than any other golf links on the island. Summer visitors to Shelter Island are constant players and the links being so extensive the game is here played in its full vigor.

West of Shelter Island, farther out in the bay, is Robin's Island, famous for hunting and fishing, and owned by the Robin's Island Gun Club. The first man of English birth who settled in New York State had the good judgment to select for his home an island in this vicinity. He purchased from the Indians, in 1639, Gardiner's Island, as it is now called, from the name of its first white owner. It is still in the possession of a member of the Gardiner family, and has about one hundred inhabitants, who are engaged in the maintenance of the estate, and in farming, gardening, and stock raising. Gardiner's Island and Block Island both lie east of Shelter Island, and well out to sea. The surrounding waters have for years been the manœuvering grounds of the Naval Reserve forces, which adds to their attractions.

SHELTER ISLAND GOLF CLUB AND SHORE

PROSPECT HOUSE AND COTTAGES, SHELTER ISLAND

THE HOTEL MANHANSET SHELTER ISLAND

ALONG THE NORTH SHORE

NE of the choicest bits of shore on the American continent is that section of Long Island termed the North Shore. It has a rich diversity of bluff and woodland along the water-front, and recedes into beautiful meadows and a fertile farming country, broken by long arms and deep bays of the Sound. The topography is wholly different from that of either the central section or the South Shore, and offers the summer resident a diversified region, in which the attractions of both water and woodland are dominant features. The many bays which indent the irregular shore-line offer not only desirable sites for cottage homes, as well as costly villas and great estates, but afford the best facilities for yachting, rowing, and fishing.

The Long Island Railroad reaches practically all the chief places on the North Shore, and through the fine local and express train service brings them into convenient and close touch with New York This division of the road, starting at Long Island City, touches Woodside and Winfield.

This is a thriving, modern, all-alive town. Near at hand is Winfield, rapidly growing into prominence because of its accessibility for those doing business in New York and Brooklyn and desiring rural homes close to the mart of commerce. Already the building contractor is

A COVE ON THE NORTH SHORE

94

on the scene, and a number of pretty cottages are always in process of erection.

Elmhurst, formerly Newtown, is one of the old villages which present many points of interest to those who value the history and associations which attach to it. Its Episcopal church has the memories of a century. The foundations were laid before Washington crossed the Delaware, and it is yet a staunch and sturdy place of worship. Its congregation was patriotic too. It was English in creed, but American in sentiment, from the good clergyman who prayed for the success of the Continental forces before the battle of Long Island, to its humblest worshiper, who fought boldly against the Hessians

ON A PLEASANT SATURDAY AFTERNOON

in that memorable struggle. Washington himself worshiped in this church, and the ill-fated André attended service there shortly before he paid the penalty of war for the treachery for which Benedict Arnold should have suffered.

Corona, a little further beyond, is the permanent residence of very many of New York's business men, and is a growing and popular town. The country roads all about are as smooth as asphalt and the cyclist finds upon them unceasing delight. There are charming drives, also, and many a happy couple have plighted a lasting troth in the moonlight of this refreshing region.

95

The town of Flushing is the largest and most important on this branch of the railroad. It is a residence town par excellence. It has a population of fourteen thousand people, many of whom do business in New York City. Some of its homes are admirable specimens of the ideal country house, sitting back in wide lawns filled with stately trees. There is a stability about the place which is typical of the substantial Long Island town; the churches are massive and imposing, and the school facilities as good as can be found anywhere, and many wealthy people live there the year through. Neither is Flushing behind the age in its out-of-door sports, and recently fine golf links have been laid out and are proving immensely popular.

A FLUSHING STREET

The residences of Flushing extend at intervals along the avenues clear to College Point, a town distant about one mile.

Whitestone, on the East River, next to College Point, has an unobstructed view of the marine procession in and out of the Sound.

East of Flushing is Bayside, vying with the others for prominence as a residence resort, and boasting the same attractive surroundings.

One of the most enjoyable sports for wheelmen is a run from Bayside to Fort Willett's Point. The roads are broad, and well kept, thus making wheeling one of the joys of life.

Some of the residences around Bayside are very tastefully built. Splendid lawns lend grace to the homes, and the roadside is lined with magnificent trees entirely overshadowing the sidewalk. The golf links, extending from Bayside almost to Douglaston, are the equal of any links in the country. The topography of the land along this division of the Long Island Railroad is rolling, and therefore eminently adapted for the game.

Douglaston, on Little Neck Bay. One does not need to go farther for satisfactory sport. Here is the home of the Little Neck clam, as succulent a morsel as the Blue Point oyster. Little Neck Bay is just east of Willett's Point, which is a prominent national military point. You may rest here for a time. An idle moment will be well repaid. Here is the great estate of W. P. Douglas. He has a lovely house upon his broad acres, and has made many improvements.

Great Neck, of which Little Neck is a neighbor, is about fourteen miles from the towers of the Brooklyn Bridge. Here are many beautiful private residences overlooking the Sound.

Here the country rises, and the bluffs make the spot picturesque. The summer home of Ex-Mayor Grace attracts by its beauty at this point, which he calls Graceland. From Great

ALONG THE SOUND SHORE NEAR GREAT NECK

97

ENTRANCE TO GRACELAND, GREAT NECK

Neck a number of fine roads diverge to various places of interest.

Manhasset, the next station, has traditions, too. Stout Miles Standish came so far, and with him a young Englishman named Davis. He was of fine stature and gentle birth, so there must have been some unusual attraction in the Indian girl who ensnared his heart. The story is as old as the region of which we speak. It has been told of other lovers in all climes, but it loses no interest because of the romantic surroundings here. The girl was loved by a young brave of the village, but she returned the affection of her white admirer, and sought to flee with him. He was faithful even unto death, and when they were pursued, with his back against the great stone upon which is graven his name, fought gallantly until they slew him. Plucking the fatal arrow from the heart of her lover, the Indian girl took her own life, and they were buried where they fell. Rugged vines and great patches of moss are on the stone near where they rest, but their names, graven upon the rock, are yet to be deciphered, and the lovers of to-day who make of the spot a favorite trysting-place, re-

VIEWS AROUND PORT WASHINGTON

peat the ancient story with hushed voices, and find a tender inspiration in recalling it.

The railroad was two years ago extended from Great Neck, through Manhasset and out upon the cape four miles to Port Washington. The completion of this line opened up a most delightful region, both to permanent residents and summer sojourners. Port Washington, the terminus of this branch of the North Side Division, is an ideal rural location, and "beautiful for situation." The hill-tops overlook the glistening Sound, with the quiet village nestling on its shore. The gentle waves rolling in from

A LONG ISLAND ROAD

the Sound ripple with laughter as they break against the beach. The roads are macadamized and well kept. From Port Washington to Sands Point Lighthouse is a most delightful trip. High trees overhang the roads and form charming avenues, giving a quiet and a restfulness not surpassed by any point on the island.

The whole country is rich and fertile; well tilled and cultivated farms and heavy timber lands abound on every hand.

Forty-eight minutes from the traffic of Broadway, from the ceaseless roar and the thunder of the city that never sleeps,

A WOODLAND ROAD

here is the restful quiet of the bird, the tree, and the flower, the peace of the sunlit water, and the ozone of the country air—a whole summer of the wheel and the camera amid rural delights that offer constant variety and change.

Port Washington is as quaint and curious as any settlement on Long Island. The entire region through which the North Side Division passes will well repay exploration for those who have never known of it.

JAMAICA TO OYSTER BAY

I T was a fine business policy which developed the Long Island Railroad. For years a region as fertile as the bottom lands of Illinois lay upon the very threshold of the metropolis of this country neglected and almost unknown. Perhaps its very proximity to New York and Brooklyn was responsible for this neglect. Human nature is apt to overlook the bounties which heaven has given it, and ungratefully sigh for more. Railroads were for far countries. They were the means of travel to lands hitherto inaccessible. The farthest point upon Long Island was in reach of the stage-coach, and all the ships that had breasted the billows of the broad Atlantic had skirted its green shores. And so the moneys of the country sent the iron horse to Mexico and laid a thousand miles of track through the Mojave desert before the complete development of the enormous latent possibilities of Long Island by the steam highway had been brought about.

Jamaica is the point at which the lines of this great highway diverge. And it is as though this little city feels its importance, and is swelling with a just pride. It has gained the recognition of adjacent Brooklyn, and has become a part of its thrift and enterprise. Its stores are commodious. It has all the conveniences and luxuries. It has schools, churches, academies, colleges, and factories, but it is essentially a residence town. One portion of it would especially attract attention, for it presents as charming a section of architectural beauty as can be found elsewhere in the East. The houses are more than costly—they make a better appeal to commendation; they are handsome, and built in excellent taste. Their owners are in business in New York City, and their homes are more accessible to the stores and places of amusement about Twenty-third Street than are those of Yonkers, Larchmont, Mt. Vernon, or New Rochelle.

As the Oyster Bay branch of railroad leaves Mineola, nine miles east of Jamaica, the ascent is gradual, until at Sea Cliff the altitude is high above the level of Long Island Sound. All the way to Oyster Bay the route is through a

AT ROSLYN

charming country unequaled for romantic beauty. The stations along the route are Roslyn, Wheatly Hills, Glen Head, Sea Cliff, Glen Cove, Nassau, Locust Valley, and Oyster Bay.

When Roslyn is reached the region upon the left becomes more precipitous, and the elevation continues sharply until the summit at Sea Cliff is attained. From the point where the line diverges at Mineola to the south is slightly rolling country, and to the north the shrubbery attains the dignity of a forest. But the entire prospect is one of verdure, forever green in its trappings of rural beauty.

A DRIVE NEAR THE BAY

103

THE WILLIAM CULLEN BRYANT HOMESTEAD, ROSLYN

Roslyn is in a gentle valley with a situation peculiarly inviting to those in search of country comforts. To mention Roslyn and make no reference to William Cullen Bryant is a profanation in the eyes of its inhabitants. Here the venerable poet made his country home; and here he gathered about him from time to time the friends of his guild, Ralph Waldo Emerson, John G. Whittier, Hamilton Mabie, and Dr. Abbott. Henry Ward Beecher was his guest, and from time to time in the cool of the summer evenings the sojourners at Roslyn have seen the national poet and the national preacher communing with nature along its shady roads. With Mr. Bryant it was a summer home of selection and not of necessity. Roslyn was the resort of his choice. His "Glossary of American Poetry" was compiled here during his leisure hours, and here some of his best verse was written.

Near at hand is Hempstead Harbor, a safe retreat for the sailing craft of the Sound. Behind the village is the highest point of ground on Long Island, from the summit of which a magnificent view is afforded for miles about. The waters of the Sound lie shimmering like a summer sea directly beneath the eye, while the rolling country makes a panorama which is unexcelled, and far to the south is a luminous region of fertile lands which supply abundantly the markets of the great city of New York. Sea Cliff, beyond, is a resort which is growing rapidly in popularity among those acquainted with its advantages. Few people as yet have a conception of its beauties. It is a commanding point, arising like a sentinel against the sky, overlooking the sheltered bay, which is unequaled for its still-water bathing. The beach at the foot of the towering cliffs is a sandy strip upon which are built the bathhouses of the hotels. Pleasure craft are innumerable. The town is

AN ARM OF THE BAY AT ROSLYN

sheltered by a dense grove which crowns the summit of the bluff, and all about lawns and flowers surrounding private cottages mark the presence of people of culture and refinement. There is music from the balconies in the evenings and the sound of the dance in the parlors of the summer hotels. Sea Cliff is becoming popular.

From Sea Cliff many interesting points may be visited. One of these is the village of Glen Cove, a thrifty and progressive town. A good business is done in Glen Cove, the establishment of the National Starch Company being located here. The product of this factory is known all over the world, and it

THE GLEN COVE SHORE

maintains in constant employment a large number of working people. Adjacent to Glen Cove is the Pratt property, an estate of eight hundred acres, magnificently located, with a frontage on Long Island Sound. On the Pratt estate is the tomb of the late Charles Pratt, in his lifetime the most prominent personage identified with Glen Cove. He located his country home upon the estate above referred to, and established a model educational school building for the town, which he designed to stand as his most enduring monument. He died before the realization of his hopes, but his sons carried out as a sacred injunction the favorite design of his lifetime, and the building was dedicated with due solemnity on May 24, 1893. The institution maintains an agricultural department which is operated upon a portion of the estate, and here the students are initiated into the best and latest researches of modern farming. Contiguous to the Pratt estate the veteran editor of the New York "Sun," recently deceased, laid out his magnificent possessions, known as "Dana Island." This beautiful property is known

THE WAYSIDE SPRING

far and wide, and the late Charles A. Dana lavished upon it a constant and unremitting care. It is as celebrated in the records of horticulture as the famous Shaw's Garden of St. Louis, and contains trees, plants, and shrubs collected from every portion of the globe. Dull care and business were never

NASSAU COUNTRY CLUB, GLEN COVE

allowed to enter this ideal spot. To Mr. Dana it was a happy valley of Rasselas. His last hours were spent here, and the estate is to be maintained in its integrity and beauty with the same reverent care as was lavished upon it by its lamented owner. This vicinity is close enough to the cities to be easily reached at all hours, and all should visit it. The train service is frequent, and many summer sojourners attend to the business of the office in New York all through the summer season, and every evening find here a period of rest and recreation. The roads all about are excellent, and wheeling is unsurpassed. In addition to all the many and varied pleasures of the water, here are always social enjoyments of the most delightful kind, and golfing is one of the most popular pastimes. The Nassau Golf Club Links are famous all over the golfing world. They extend from Nassau almost to Locust Valley, and their situation is superb, the views being particularly far-reaching and varied. The Long Island Railroad runs special trains to and from New York and Brooklyn to accommodate players.

The next point of interest is Locust Valley, a place of admirable location. Numerous boarding-houses providing an excellent cuisine are located here. The views are fine, and a morning stroll at this point along the shores of the Sound will well repay the visitor. The

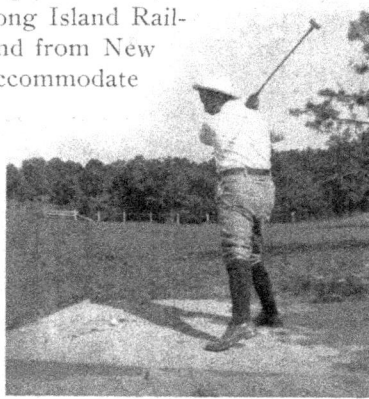

GOLFING AT GLEN COVE

107

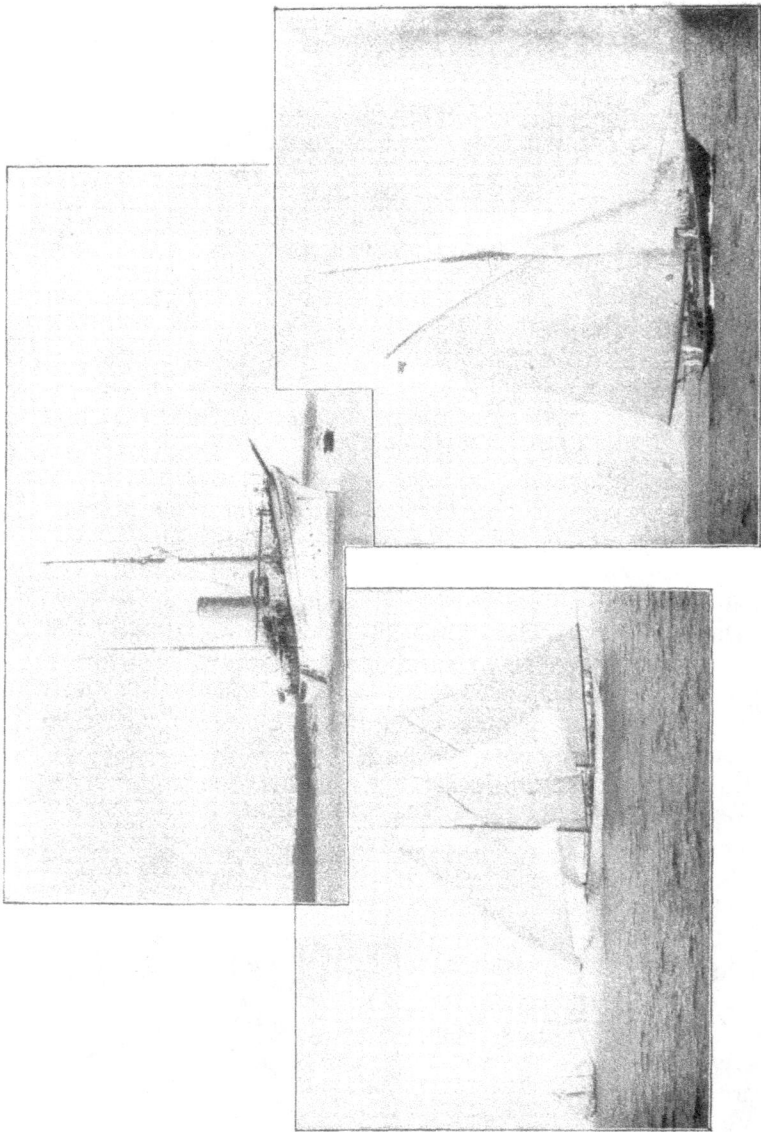

ON THE SOUND OFF GLEN COVE

Connecticut outline is plainly discernible in the distance. There is no malaria nor mosquitoes. Here is located the Friends' Academy, justly celebrated for its thorough curriculum. Students come from near and far, and many a man of prominence owes his success in life to the habits of earnest study acquired at this admirable school. It is more than a century old, and in the beginning was endowed by Gideon Frost, standing to-day a monument to his lofty public spirit. The surrounding country is one of the most fertile on Long Island.

YACHTING ON OYSTER BAY

Here are raised vast quantities of asparagus. The roads hereabouts are long and gleaming white pathways over which the cyclists may speed as on a race-course. Here as elsewhere throughout this beautiful country will be found good fishing, hunting, and sailing. At Bayville, which is a short distance from Locust Valley, upon the water-front, is located the institution known as the "Downing Vacation House." It is an establishment for the benefit of working women, a beautiful expression of the charity of our public-spirited people. It is known rather for the good it has done than the appearance which it presents, and many a deserving woman remembers with heartfelt gratitude a summer of delightful and healthful outing which it has afforded her.

The terminus of this branch of the railroad is Oyster Bay. Its earliest inhabitant named it well, although for nearly four centuries he has slumbered with his fathers. It is a charming summer resort, much affected by a fashionable class from New York, although comfortable hotels and boarding places can be found here. Oyster Bay has a large number of splendid private cottages, and the place is at once striking and modern and quaint and antique. It is the centre of fashion and wealth, and one of America's most attractive waterside resorts. Its position makes it a favorite place for pleasure craft, and here is found the home of the Seawanhaka Yacht Club. The club-house is an imposing structure, splendidly situated at the very entrance of the bay. A green lawn, bisected with wide walks, slopes gently up to the broad verandas, which overlook the waters, and here, during the yachting season, can be found a

CLUBHOUSE AND DOCK, SEAWANHAKA YACHT CLUB, OYSTER BAY

goodly assemblage of fair women and brave men. Many a regatta takes place before its windows, and the view from its front is unsurpassed. Amongst its many other special features and particular advantages Oyster Bay prides itself upon having within its borders the summer home of Governor Roosevelt. The village of Oyster Bay is an attractive one. Its history is identified with that of the Quaker sect, who for a century and a half practically dominated it. At the period of the first settlement of this country this spot was much coveted

VIEWS AT OYSTER BAY, SHOWING RESIDENCE OF GOVERNOR ROOSEVELT

A LONG ISLAND FARM

by the English, but their efforts at colonization were frustrated by a determined resistance on the part of the Dutch, who were then in possession. In 1653 a colony of persons from Sandwich, Mass., purchased from the Matinecock Indians a tract of land which forms a portion of the present site, and established a settlement there. It is related by Prime in his history of Long Island that in 1672, when George Fox, the Quaker preacher, visited this country, he went to Oyster Bay to attend a "half-yearly meeting," and to thrill the audience there assembled with his earnest and rugged eloquence. From Oyster Bay, as straight as the line of railroad between Moscow and St. Petersburg, runs "the great, broad highway leading down to Massapequa on the other side of Long Island, a run unequaled for cyclists, and many a good record has been made on this route." Amidst its many other pleasures Oyster Bay has kept fully abreast with the times and has established its own golf links, which are attractively laid out and very popular.

FROM HICKSVILLE TO PORT JEFFERSON AND WADING RIVER

THE Port Jefferson branch of the Long Island Railroad runs through as delightful a country as can be found in any of the regions of summer resort. This branch of the railroad leaves the main line at Hicksville, and, running north to Syosset, continues a northeasterly course to Huntington by way of Cold Spring Harbor. The topography of Long Island, as has been described before, is one of uplands and hills to the north, receding in a succession of undulating plains to the fertile farming lands of the south. The Port Jefferson branch of the railroad runs through the picturesque hills of the north amidst foliage, groves, and the environ-

AN OLD HOMESTEAD

ment of vine and flower which makes the entire vicinity a
natural park of surpassing beauty.

Cold Spring Harbor, the first point of interest, is a quaint
and attractive village, situated upon a lovely bay of the same
name, which is one of the noblest estuaries of the Sound. The
surroundings are as charming as those of the Lake of Como.
The shores at times are wide lawns of velvet, sloping gradually
back into broad parks
of green to an elevation
overlooking the waters
for many miles.

Excellent conveyances can be found at
the station at all times
to carry the traveler to
the village, at which he
may pass an entire summer with an interest
which will endure to
the end. The ride itself
is a splendid introduction to the country. For three miles
the roadway is an
arcade of green, the
tops of the trees
meeting in a bower
above the highway.
To the left are three
lakes, and here the
State has located
one of its principal fish hatcheries,

COLD SPRING HARBOR

the product of which reaches many millions a year and serves
to bountifully replenish the waters of the Sound and vicinity
with a constantly increasing store of the finny tribes.

At Cold Spring Harbor the Brooklyn Biological Laboratory has established a summer course of study, and many
eminent scholars lecture there on appropriate subjects. Students from the best families of the State attend in large numbers, making of this antique village a modern college town.

Like many of the venerable seaports of Long Island, Cold Spring Harbor was once the seat of an extensive oil industry. Scores of arctic whalers were fitted out at this point for their perilous voyages to the north, and among the inhabitants of the village are yet to be found numbers of old salts, those rugged and hardy characters of the Eastern shipping population which made the American seaman typical the world over.

From Cold Spring Harbor to Huntington is a brief journey. Huntington is one of the most important towns upon this branch of the railroad, and here the summer sojourner can procure for himself the more pretentious comforts of an outing in addition to the usual accompaniments of a summer stay in the country. Well-equipped stores supply all the auxiliaries of the hunt, the fishing excursion, the sailing party, and cycling tour. There are comfortable hotels and fine boarding-houses also, while the surroundings bear substantial evidence of thrift and progress. Handsome private

BATHING AT HUNTINGTON

cottages abound in the vicinity, and a number of prominent people have established a summer colony here. In order to better accommodate these cottages and the citizens, the Long Island Railroad has constructed a trolley line from the station to the further end of the village, which is a very great acquisition.

At Huntington the patriotic citizens have reared a memorial to commemorate one of the most eventful and pathetic incidents of our history. A massive stone, appropriately carved, tells the tragic story of Nathan Hale, the youthful martyr to American patriotism. This young man, acting under the direct command of General Washington, penetrated, in disguise, the British lines for the purpose of procuring information for the Continental Army as to the movements and works of the British regulars. The duties of a spy were repugnant to his high spirit, but, with that faith which marked the character of so many of his associates in the trying times at the birth of this republic, he went to his duty and his death with neither protest nor resentment. After he had accomplished his mission and was returning to the State of Connecticut to make his report, he was detected by the treachery of a Tory

THE NATHAN HALE MEMORIAL AT HUNTINGTON

farmer and captured by the enemy. His fate was sealed. Taken to the city of New York, he was speedily hanged, dying with a fortitude that has made his name immortal in the annals of the country for which he sacrificed his life. One of the noblest sentiments of the famous American sculptor Mac-Monnies finds expression in the statue of bronze which was erected by the Sons of the American Revolution in the City Hall Park of New York—a majestic and pathetic figure of this noble American youth.

VIEWS IN HUNTINGTON

Huntington has, in addition to the monument to Hale, a public library which has been reared to the sacred memory of the soldiers who died for the Union. The beginning of this tract of country for American record was in 1646, when Governor Eaton, of New Haven, purchased it from the Indians. Settlers from New England formed a colony there, and laid the foundation for the substantial population which now welcomes the summer visitor with true rural hospitality. There is an admirable academy at Huntington. The prevailing religious sect was the Presbyterian, and they are in possession of a historic site for their church, which was first erected in 1784. This is the successor of a building constructed in 1715, and afterwards used by the English soldiers as a barracks and hospital, and abandoned by them upon their evacuation of the town. A number of New York and Brooklyn men have built handsome residences in this vicinity, and there are excellent roads upon which bicycling is very popular.

Centreport, of which Greenlawn is the railroad station, is a place well situated for a summer stay. It is essentially a rural village, tucked away in one of the most picturesque portions of the hills. It is an ideal spot for the hunter and the angler. Good boarding-houses abound, and rates are very low.

ALONG A NORTH SHORE ROAD

SCENE AT NORTHPORT

Beyond is Northport, beautifully situated upon a body of water which is a portion of Huntington Bay. It is a safe harbor, in which, in former times, many vessels of importance were constructed. To-day it is an enterprising, active place of much commercial importance. One of its chief industries is

RASSAPAQUE CLUB, SMITHTOWN

119

the Edward Thompson Publishing Co., one of the largest law publishing houses in the United States, employing several hundred people.

Kings Park, the station beyond Northport, is a place where Dr. Muhlenburg established a number of years ago the institutions which have since been associated with his name. It is known more familiarly in New York under the name of St. Johnland. The climate in summer at this point is unsurpassed for health and bracing vigor. Despite its hilly character, this region has many thrifty and prosperous farmers and a substantial rural population of an intelligent and progressive character.

WYANDANCH CLUBHOUSE, SMITHTOWN

Smithtown is the site of the homestead of Theodore Smith, of anti-revolutionary fame. Near here the Brooklyn Gun Club purchased a large tract of land, and close at hand are two trout ponds of some twelve acres in extent. Here also are the Rassapaque and Wyandanch clubhouses. They are erected upon the Nissequogue River, and are two of the best-appointed clubhouses along the shores of the Sound.

St. James is fortunate in its situation. The Long Island Sound with all its beauty of an inland lake lazily ebbs and flows at the foot of this pretty village. Many summer residences, costly and attractive, have been erected here within the past few years. The Sound affords ample boating and bathing facilities, and the golf links are a never-ending source of pleasure. The entire district is composed of high and beautiful rolling land.

The country traversed by the Long Island Railroad has few prettier points than that which surrounds Setauket. This village is well beyond the evidences of the city, being fifty-five miles from the Hudson River. The country changes somewhat in character here, being a succession of hills and dales, but the highways are at all times excellent. The farmhouses

PORT JEFFERSON HARBOR

are substantial, but antique. They are relics of the past century, but they were stoutly built with rafters of oak. The Sound at this point is beautiful. Numerous inlets indent the shores, and small estuaries penetrate far to the interior. The snipe hunting is superb.

Port Jefferson, the next station beyond Setauket, is an important place, long known for its shipyards. They are still maintained, and numerous crafts are here repaired and fitted out for their voyages in the coast trade. Port Jefferson was an admirable vantage point during the Revolutionary War, and here was fitted out a vessel upon which Paul Jones achieved a portion of his reputation. Captain Kidd rendezvoused at Port Jefferson, and at this point murdered two English officers of the frigate "Nahant." It was from Port Jefferson that the ill-fated whaler "Greenland" sailed upon her last voyage, and here two vessels of the British fleet anchored shortly before the battle of Long Island. The harbor of Port Jef-

SURF AT ROCKY POINT. LIFE SAVING STATION MARINE

ferson is one of the safest on the Sound, and its shores are delightfully attractive for summer bathing. The village has good hotels and good boarding-houses, and yachts are for hire at reasonable prices during the summer months.

Sailing parties often go from Port Jefferson for an extended tour along the New England shores, stopping at various points of interest to the east and north. The entire country from Port Jefferson to Wading River, the terminus of this branch of the railroad, is admirably adapted for summer recreation, as the land is high and healthy, and affords an infinite variety of beautiful water views.

The ample facilities offered by the Long Island Railroad are by no means the only transportation advantages this famous old harbor possesses; for daily trips are made by steamer from Port Jefferson to Bridgeport directly across the Long Island Sound, bringing into easy touch the entire New England coast line.

CONTENTS

CONTENTS – Continued

Manhattan Beach

Swept by Ocean Breezes

Manhattan Beach Hotel

European Plan

T. F. SILLECK, Manager

Oriental Hotel

American Plan

JOSEPH P. GREAVES, Manager

Grand Concerts, Favorite Operas, Brilliant Fireworks, Ocean Bathing, Sailing, Fishing, Bicycling

Forty Minutes from New York
Temperature Seldom Varies from 70 Degrees

For Further Particulars see Pages 20 to 25

OFFICES OF THE COMPANY, 192 Broadway

New York City, N. Y.

WM. SELLERS & CO.

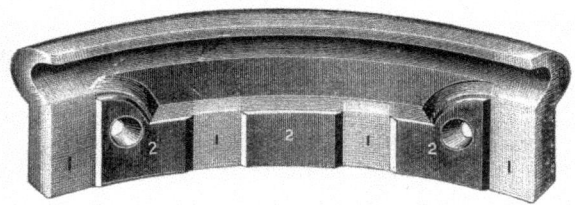

The Safety Car Heating and Lighting Company

160 Broadway, New York

❧

Pintsch System Car and Buoy Lighting

This Company controls in the United States and Canada the celebrated Pintsch System of Car and Buoy Lighting. It is economical, safe, efficient, and approved by Railway Managers and the Light-House Board of the United States, and has received the highest awards for excellence at the World's Expositions at Moscow, Vienna, St. Petersburg, London, Berlin, Paris, Chicago and Atlanta. Ninety-seven thousand cars, three thousand two hundred locomotives, and one thousand buoys are equipped with this light.

Street Railway Lines

This system of Lighting has been adopted by the Broadway and Third Avenue Cable Lines of New York; the North and West Chicago, and the Chicago City Railway Lines of Chicago; the Olive Street Railway of St. Louis; the Columbus Central Electric Line of Columbus, Ohio; the Metropolitan Street Railway of Kansas City, and the Denver Cable Lines of Denver, Colorado. These roads have three thousand cars equipped with this light.

Car Heating

By STEAM JACKET SYSTEM, HOT WATER CIRCULATION RETURN AND REGULATING DIRECT STEAM SYSTEMS

Automatic Steam Couplers

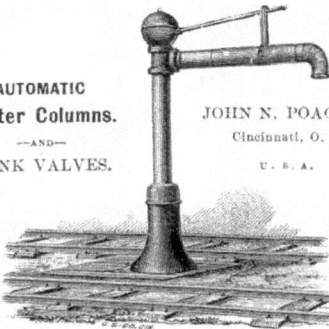

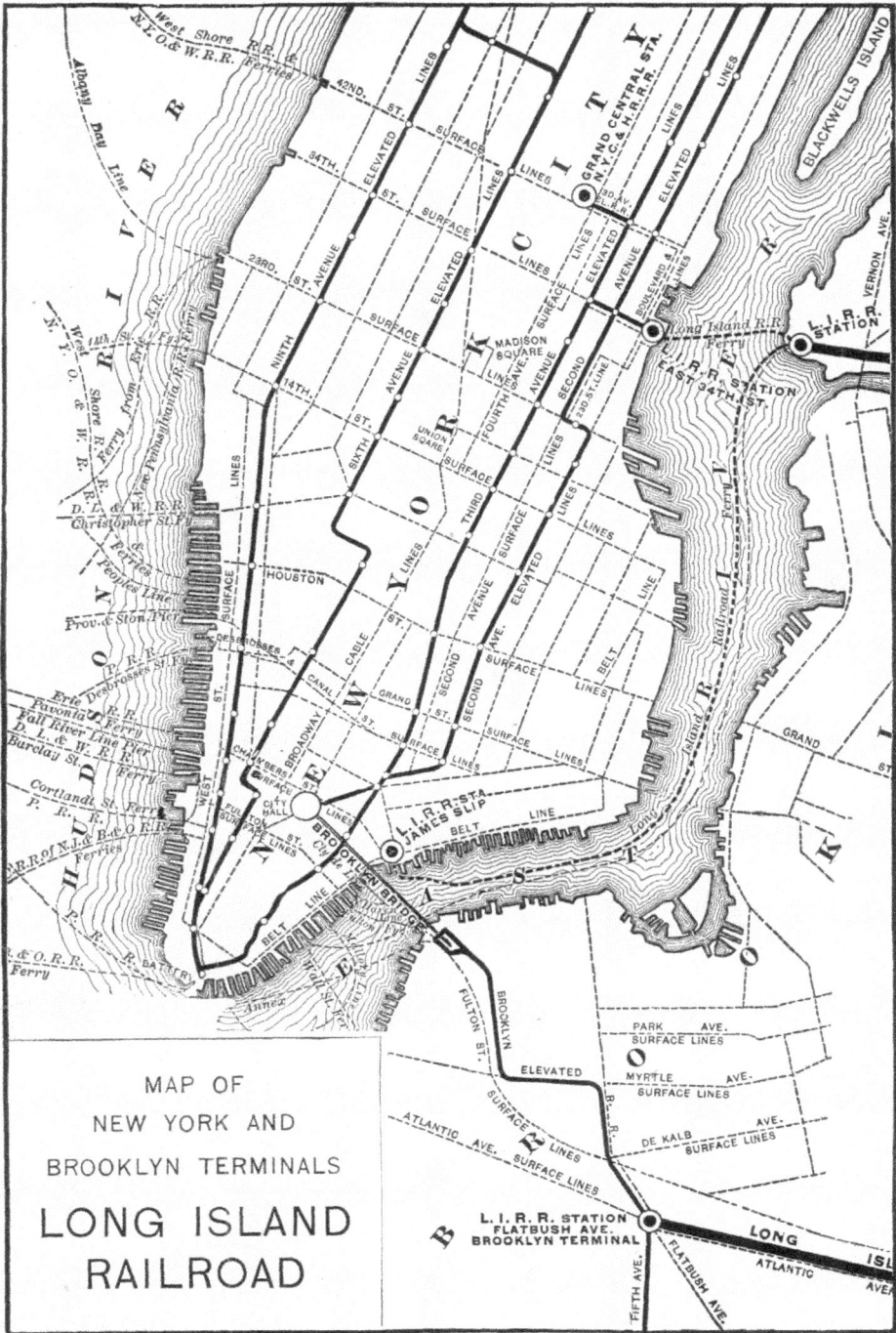

MAP OF
NEW YORK AND
BROOKLYN TERMINALS

LONG ISLAND
RAILROAD

www.ingramcontent.com/pod-product-compliance
Lightning Source LLC
Chambersburg PA
CBHW080514110426
42742CB00017B/3107